Nubian Proverbs

Dotawo ▸
Monographs

4

Dotawo ▸ Monographs

Series Editors   Alexandros Tsakos
                   Vincent W.J. van Gerven Oei

Design   Vincent W.J. van Gerven Oei
Typeset in 10/12 Skolar PE and Sawarda Nubian.

Cover image   Courtyard, Dongola region
                   Photo by Vincent W.J. van Gerven Oei, 2016.

Dotawo ▸ is an imprint of punctum books

NUBIAN PROVERBS (FADIJJA/MAHAS). Copyright © 2022 Maher Habbob. This work carries a Creative Commons BY-NC-SA 4.0 International license, which means that you are free to copy and redistribute the material in any medium or format, and you may also remix, transform, and build upon the material, as long as you clearly attribute the work to the authors (but not in a way that suggests the authors or punctum books endorses you and your work), you do not use this work for commercial gain in any form whatsoever, and that for any remixing and transformation, you distribute your rebuild under the same license. http://creativecommons.org/licenses/by-nc-sa/4.0/

First published in 2022 by Dotawo,
an imprint of punctum books, Earth, Milky Way.
https://punctumbooks.com/

ISBN-13: 978-1-68571-018-7 (print); 978-1-68571-019-4 (ePDF)
LCCN: 2022930855
DOI: 10.53288/0346.1.00

Maher Habbob
**Nubian Proverbs
(Fadijja/Mahas)**

Contents

Introduction · · · · · · · · · · · · · · · · · · · 15
Proverbs · 23
References · 145

Proverbs give a wonderful insight into a culture.

To some African ethnic groups proverbs are not explained but rather they are self-explanatory. Their meaning is straightforward. In fact, proverbs in a nutshell communicate truth. Truth is sometimes bitter and can be corrupted by logical grammatical usage in language. Nevertheless proverbs spare the corruption of truth.

– Okeke Onyeka Augustine, Tanzania

*Dedicated to
Abubakr Sidahmed and Gerald Lauche,
my friends, guides, and compass.
Your sudden death made me lose my Nubian direction,
may your souls rest in peace.*

Acknowledgments

This first edition of *Nubian Proverbs (Fadijja/Mahas)* could not have been written without the advice and assistance of many friends whom I would like to thank. First of all, much gratitude to my mother Souad Bahr Othman, the late Awada Ali Othman, the late Zainab Jamal Salim, Saida Awad, and the late Taha Zayar, from whom I collected these proverbs in my village Tōmās wa Afye. Many thanks to my friends Abdel Nasser Youssef, Fouad Akoud, Marcus Jaeger, and Gerald Lauche for their support and discussions whether in personal meetings or via the internet, my friend Alaa Khaled who previously published some of my articles in his unique and pioneering magazine *Amkenah* (*Places*). I would also like to thank my friends Rami Yahya and the writer Samar Nour, who did their best to find an accurate publisher for the Arabic version of this text. Many thanks and gratitude to the writers Yahya Mukhtar and Ahmed Abu Khnaijar with whom I discussed possible publishing houses and the available alternatives. I would further like to thank my friends Asma Abu Bakr, Hind Bakr, Hanan Mahfouz, Rehab Salih, Elizabeth Smith, Faisal Al-Mawsali, Hussein Othman, Muhammad Al-Ansari, and Muhammad Gaber, who encouraged me to finish this book, Dr. Muddathir Salim who put me on this path, and special thanks to the writers Haggag Addoul and Sabri Yahya who supplied me with books from their Nubian library, before I had my own, in particular Ibrahim Shaarawi's book *Al-khorafa wa al-ostura fi plead al-nuba* [*Myth and Legend in the Land of Nubia*], published in 1984, which opened the doors to the amazing world of Nubian oral heritage. I also thank all those who followed and read what I used to collect and write about proverbs, discussing with me about how to write them, whether I followed their advice or not, my friends Mohiuddin Salih, Safwat Muhammad Sharif, and Dr. Ahmed Sukarno. Finally I want to express my gratitude and love to my wife, children, mother, uncle, and sisters for their continued support and patience.

Maher Habbob
Tōmās wa Afye

Introduction

In the 1995/96 academic year, twenty-five Egyptian Nubian students of the Faculty of Social Work in Aswan were recruited by Dr. Muddathir Salim to complete a brief Nubian ethnological survey, largely restricted to the area of New Nubia, over a period of several months. They documented Egyptian Nubian culture and heritage, among them proverbs, tales, lullabies, marriage customs, and *moulid* and mourning songs, as well as models of Nubian clothes, jewelry, and houses. Unfortunately their work remained incomplete and unpublished.

During this project, I collected about fifty Fadijja proverbs. Together with two female students, Walaa Salah al-Din from the village of Dahmit, who collected forty-two Kenzi proverbs, and Sanaa Gaber from village of Al-Maliki, who found nine Arabic proverbs, I continued working on Fadijja and Mattokki/Kenzi proverbs until the end of 1999, at which point I had collected about 365 Fadijja proverbs. This project turned into an obsession and a personal race to collect and document the heritage and folklore of Nubia. Nowadays (2020), my collection contains about 2,000 proverbs, in addition to dozens of tales, songs, and photographs.

A Note on the Presentation

The five hundred proverbs in this book are presented in three ways:

1. In Nubian script[1]: ⲅⲓⲛⲇⲓ ⲇⲁⲅⲓ ⲫⲉⲛⲧⲓ ⲕⲁⲙⲙⲟⲩⲛ.
2. Transliteration in Latin alphabet: *Gindi jaagi fenti kammun.*

The transliteration follows the table on the next page:

---

1 Following the method presented in Mukhtar Khalil Kabbara, *Nubiinga sikkir faaywa?* [How Do We Write the Nubian Language?], 1st edn. (Cairo: Nubian Studies and Documentation Center, 1997) and *Nubiinga kull* [*Learning the Nubian Language*] (Cairo: Nubian Studies and Documentation Center, 1999).

Nubian character	Approximate phonetic value	Transliteration
ⲁ	[a]	*a*
ⲁ̄	[a:]	*aa*
ⲃ	[b]	*b*
ⲅ	[g]	*g*
ⲇ	[d]	*d*
ⲉ	[ɛ]	*e*
ⲉ̄	[ɛ:]	*ee*
ϭ	[tʃ]	*c*
ⲍ	[z]	*z*
ⲓ	[i]	*i*
ⲓ̄	[i:]	*ii*
ϊ	[j]	*y*
ⲕ	[k]	*k*
ⲗ	[l]	*l*
ⲙ	[m]	*m*
ⲛ	[n]	*n*
ⲟ	[ɔ]	*o*
ⲟ̄	[ɔ:]	*oo*
ⲟⲩ	[u]	*u*
ⲟ̄ⲩ̄	[u:]	*uu*
ⲡ	[p]	*p*
ⲣ	[r]	*r*
ⲥ	[s]	*s*
ⲧ	[t]	*t*
ⲫ	[f]	*f*
ⲱ	[w]	*w*
ϣ	[ʃ]	*sh*
ϩ	[h]	*h*

Nubian character	Approximate phonetic value	Transliteration
ϩ	[dʒ]	j
⸋	[ŋ]	ng
⸌	[ɲ]	ny

3. A literal English translation: "Whoever is afraid of thorns will not eat dates."
4. An indication as to when the proverb is used: To those who want to get something, yet fear the troubles that may come.

This collection of proverbs is loosely organized into several semantic domains, such as work, upbringing, agriculture, and marriage & family. The basis for classification is the proverb's literal meaning. It may belong to a different semantic domain, as well.

Writing Nobíin: A Brief Chronology

Three orthographies have been involved in writing the Nobíin (Fadijja/Mahas) language, namely Nubian, Latin, and Arabic. In the Christian era of the Nubian kingdoms, a native script was derived from Greek, Coptic, and Meroitic scripts to write the Old Nubian language. If we accept the notion that considers Old Nubian as a direct ancestor of Nobíin,[2] then perhaps the 8th century CE was the first time for Nobíin to appear in writing. Stricker endorses Griffith's view when he writes that Old Nubian is the "medieval phase of the language now spoken between Korosko and Hannak."[3] All Old Nubian literary works, both literary and documentary, are written in the distinctive Nubian script.

Nobíin in Latin script appeared centuries later. Here we are going to make a panoramic review with a particular focus on works of a literary nature. A tentative vocabulary list of Nobíin was made by Burckhardt.[4] De Cadalvene and de Breuvery[5] also included a vocabulary list in their survey of Egypt and Turkey. The transliteration systems employed in these works reflected the traditions pertaining to the respective countries to which each belonged. For instance, De Cadalvene and De Breuvery maintain the characters /a/, /e/, /i/, /o/,

---

[2] F.Ll. GRIFFITH, "Some Old Nubian Christian Texts," *The Journal of Theological Studies* 10, no. 40 (1909): pp. 545-551, at p. 545.
[3] B.H. STRICKER, "A Study in Medieval Nubian," *Bulletin of the School of Oriental Studies, University of London* 10, no. 2 (1940): pp. 439-454.
[4] J.L. BURCKHARDT, *Travels in Nubia* (London: John Murray, 1819).
[5] E. de CADALVENE and J. de BREUVERY, *L'Égypte et la Turquie, de 1829 à 1836*, Vol. 2: *Égypte et Nubie* (Paris, 1836).

and /ou/ (for /u/) for short as well as for long vowels. It is only after Lepsius introduced his notational system in 1853 that modifications of Latin scripts began showing systematic and standardized orientations that have culminated in the International Phonetic Alphabet (IPA). A real Nobíin literary work written in Latin script did not appear for more than two decades. The Gospel of Mark, translated into Nobíin and typeset in Latin script, was published in Berlin in 1860.[6] It was translated in Cairo under the supervision of Lepsius by a Sudanese Nubian named Hasan, who was from the village of "Seree" (i.e., Serre, without identifying whether it was Serre East or West).[7] From that time until the first decade of the 20th century, many editions of this Nobíin gospel appeared. Years later, Reinisch[8] published his Nubian-German and German-Nubian dictionary, where Nobíin is represented in what seemed to Reinisch as two distinct dialects, "Fadisch" and "Mahassi." In fact he treats Andaandi/Dongolawi, Mattokki/Kenzi, Fadijja, and Mahas as dialects of a single Nile Nubian language. A year later, the impressively comprehensive work of Lepsius[9] on Nubian grammar appeared containing a Nubian-German and German-Nubian dictionary, and the translation of the Gospel of Mark in Nobíin. Latin script was used for writing Nobíin. In 1888, Rochemonteix produced his book of Nubian tales, which contained nine tales in Nobíin written in Latin script, with their French translations. For some reason, one of these Nobíin tales was produced in Arabic script.[10] The Nobíin Gospel of Mark appeared in Cairo in 1899 in Arabic script.[11] By then the Old Nubian manuscripts had been being identified as Nubian by Schäfer and Schmidt,[12] to be properly deciphered and extensively studied by Griffith,[13] and later more analyzed and criticized by Zyhlarz.[14] In 1913, Hans Abel's book[15] appeared, which contained small examples of Nobíin folktales with their German translations and explanations and a glossary at the end using the Latin script.

6 G. Lauche, "A Contribution to the History of K.R. Lepsius, Translation of the Gospel of Mark into Mahas," The International Conference of Meroitic & Nubian Studies, Nice, 1996.
7 Ibid.
8 L. Reinisch, Die Nuba-sprache (Vienna: Wilhelm Braumüller, 1879).
9 K.R. Lepsius, Nubische Grammatik: Mit einer Einleitung über die Völker und Sprachen Afrikas (Berlin: Wilhelm Hertz, 1880).
10 M. de Rochemonteix, Quelques contes nubiens (Cairo, 1888).
11 K.R. Lepsius, [The Gospel According to St. Mark Translated into the Nubian language: An Edition of R. Lepsius' version, Transliterated into Arabic characters by Theodor Irrisch] (Alexandria, 1899).
12 H. Schäfer and K. Schmidt, "Die ersten Bruchstücke christlicher Literatur in altnubischer Sprache," Sitzungsberichte der Königlichen Preussischen Akademie der Wissenschaften 43 (1906): pp. 774–785.
13 F.Ll. Griffith, The Nubian Texts of the Christian Period (Berlin: Verlag der Königlichen Akademie der Wissenschaften, 1913).
14 E. Zyhlarz, Grundzüge der Nubischen Grammatik im Christlichen Frühmittelalter (Altnubisch) (Leipzig: Deutsche Morgenländische Gesellschaft, 1928).
15 H. Abel, Eine Erzählung im Dialekt von Ermenne (Nubien) (Leipzig, 1913).

A few decades later, in 1955, Mutwalli Badr published his first book on Nobíin,[16] with some excerpts from the Andaandi/Dongolawi-Mattokki/Kenzi language and a vocabulary of Nobíin. He used both Latin and Arabic scripts for writing Nobíin. By this he initiated and launched a new era for writing Nobíin using Arabic script in a purely secular fashion in contrast to the missionary productions of the Gospel of Mark. The Latin script was also used by Abd Al-Rahman Ayoub in his study of the verbal system of the Fadijja dialect of Nobíin,[17] where he includes in the appendix fifteen pieces, mostly folktales. A little later Latin script was also used by Bell in his publication on Nubian place-names in the geographical region known as the "Belly of Stones," extending southwards from the Second Cataract in the middle of the Nobíin-speaking region.[18] In 1978, Mutwalli Badr produced his book on Nobíin proverbs, using the Arabic script for writing Nobíin.[19] In the same year, although it appeared as undated, his unprecedented Nobíin primer appeared with Latin script as the means of writing.[20] This Arabic–Latin dualism of writing characterizes all his works.

The decade of the 1990s witnessed a revival of the Nubian script for writing Nobíin but the fruit did not ripen until late in the nineties. By the turn of the twenty-first century, the script has become the choice of a considerable number of Nubian intellectuals in Sudan and Egypt as well.[21] This surge was initiated by an article by Old Nubian scholar Gerald M. Browne.[22] Within two decades his researches and publications on Old Nubian language amounted to more than sixty titles. The legacy of Latin script continued with Simon[23] publishing Andaandi and Nobíin songs and Roland Werner with his book of Nobíin grammar which included his own presentation of the primer of Mutwalli Badr.[24]

Meanwhile, Mohyi al-Din Sherif (Muhyi al-Dīn Sharīf) finished his manuscript of a Fadijja primer in Latin script "for Eng-

---

16   Muhammad Mutwalli BADR, *Al-lugha al-Nubiyya* [*Study in Nubian Language*] (Cairo: Dar misr lil-tiba, 1955).
17   Abd al-Rahman AYOUB, *The Verbal System in a Dialect of Nubian* (Khartoum: Sudan Research Unit, University of Khartoum, 1968).
18   Herman BELL, *Place-names in the Belly of Stones* (Khartoum: Sudan Research Unit, University of Khartoum, 1970).
19   Muhammad Mutwalli BADR, *Hikam wa amthāl al-nuba* [*Anecdotes and Proverbs of Nubia*] (Khartoum: Institute of African & Asian Studies (IAAS), University of Khartoum, 1978).
20   Muhammad Mutwalli BADR, *Igra bi al-nubiyya* (*Nubiin nog gery*) [*Read in Nubian*] (Khartoum: Institute of African & Asian Studies (IAAS), University of Khartoum, [1978]).
21   M.J. HASHIM. *Contribution of Nubian Language Speakers to the Development of Their Writing System: Insights Arising from Nubian Literacy Classrooms*. PhD Thesis, School of Language and Area Studies, University of Portsmouth, 2006.
22   G.M. BROWNE, "Notes on Old Nubian," *Bulletin of American Society of Papyrologists* 16, no. 4 (1979): pp. 249–256.
23   A. SIMON, ed., *Nordsudan: Musik der Nubier* (Berlin: Musikethnologische Abteilung, Museum für Völkerkunde Berlin, 1980).
24   R. WERNER, *Grammatik des Nobíin (Nilnubisch)* (Hamburg: Helmut Buske, 1987).

lish speakers."[25] A year later, in 1996, the publication of the Nobíin-German Dictionary of Mukhtār Khalīl (Kabbāra)[26] came out using the Nubian script, which was the launching point for a new era. In 1997, Al-Hādi Hāshim & Wheeler (a.k.a. A. Cartwright) finished publishing their Nobíin primer in Latin script.[27] Hāshim & Wheeler expressed their wish to use the Nubian script, if software was provided. A year later, in 1997, Mukhtār Khalīl produced the first teaching book for the Nobíin alphabet using the Nubian script. The book is not a primer *per se*, but rather a book that introduces the Old Nubian characters so as to be used in writing Nobíin. Although the book is mostly about Nobíin, some of the exercises deal with Mattokki/Kenzi and Andaandi/Dongolawi. In 1998, Ahmed Sokarno Abdel-Hafiz published a book on how to write both Nobíin and Andaandi/Dongolawi–Mattokki/Kenzi using an Arabic-based script; two glossaries of were added as appendices.[28] The same year also witnessed the publication of the English/Arabic Andaandi/Dongolawi-Mattokki/Kenzi and Nobíin dictionary of Sunbāj where a Latin-based script was used for writing Nubian.[29] Also in 1998, a workshop on both Nile Nubian languages was organized in Cairo by the Nubian Studies and Documentation Centre. The result of this workshop was intended to be a primer for teaching both Nobíin and Andaandi/Dongolawi–Mattokki/Kenzi simultaneously in one book. Due to the overwhelming number of mistakes a second edition of the publication appeared in 2002, using the Nubian script for writing the two Nubian languages while Arabic script was used for the explanation. In 2005, al-Hādi Hasan Hāshim & Roland Werner published their collection of Nobíin folktales with an English translation, using Latin script to write Nobíin.

This brief overview shows that the writing of Nobíin language has a long history. In fact Meroitic and Nobíin (i.e., Old Nubian) are among the first languages of purely African origin to be written. Three scripts (Nubian, Latin, and Arabic) have been involved in the process of writing Nubian languages. One would assume that this history would have led to some sort of standardization for each script. While this was arguably achieved long ago for Old Nubian

---

25 M. Sherif [Mohyi al-Din Sharif], *Fadijja Nubian Language Lessons: For English Speakers*, unpublished manuscript, Cairo, 1995.
26 Mokhtar Khalil [Kabbara], *Wörterbuch der Nubischen Sprache (Fadidja/Mahas-Dialekt)* (Warsaw, 1996).
27 Al-Hādi Hasan Hāshim and A.L. Wheeler [A. Cartwright], *Nobinga Kull* [*Learn Nubian*] (Khartoum: Nobatia Society, 1997).
28 Ahmed Sokarno Abdel-Hafiz, *Nahw muhawala li kitabat alugha al-Nubiyya* [*Toward an Attempt to Write the Nubian Language*] (Cairo, 1998).
29 Y. Sunbaj, *Al-qamus al-nubi* [*The Nubian Dictionary: English/Arabic/Kenzi-Dongolese and Nobiin*]. Cairo, 1998.

(8th century to 15th century CE), a generally accepted orthography has not yet been adopted by modern Nubians.[30]

---

[30] M.J. Hashim, *Nubian Orthography* (Cairo: Nubian Studies & Documentation Centre, 2008).

Proverbs

(1)

ⲅoyⲇⲇo ⲁⲅıɴ ⲙoyⲡTı ⲱⲁⲣⲁⲱⲁTTⲁ.
Guddo aagin murti warawatta.
He who sits on the ground has the fastest running horse.

    [Used to ridicule someone of many words and little action.]

(2)

Ƅⲁⱬⲁⲣⲣⲁ ⲅōɴ ⲥⲁɴTē oⲕⲕⲁⲫīɴⲁ.
Baharra goon santee okkafiina.
Even rivers have a pot/amount.

    [An advice to save and not to waste.]

(3)

ⲥeⲅeⲇ ⲙıꞔoyɴɴı? ⲕⲁⲕⲕēⲅ oyɴɴıɴⲁ.
Seged mingunni? Kakkeeg unnina.
What does scorpion give birth to? Small scorpions.

    [Bad temper is transmitted from one generation to another.]

(4)

ⲙⲁⲣⲧⲓ ⲇⲟⲕⲕⲓⲛ ⲫⲁ̄ ⲗⲁ ⲇⲟ̄ⲩⲙⲟⲩⲛ.
Marti jokkin faa la juumun.
Water will not go to the basins until the channel is full.

[Advice to await your proper turn.]

(5)

ⲫⲉ̄ⲱⲉ̄ ⲟⲩⲫⲫⲓ ⲁⲙⲁⲛⲅⲁ ⲕⲉ̄ⲣⲕⲓⲙⲟⲩⲛ.
Feeshee uffi amannga keerkimun.
The broken hopper[1] does not raise water.

[Said about someone or something defective that will not complete the work.]

(6)

ⲙⲟⲅⲟⲣⲣⲁ ⲅⲟ̄ⲛ ⲥⲁ̄ⲙⲉ̄ ⲫⲉϊⲁ ⲫⲓ̄ⲛ.
Mogorra goon saamee feya fiin.
Even a billy goat has a beard.

[What counts is personality, not appearance.]

(7)

ⲅⲟⲩⲱⲱⲁⲗ ⲅⲟ̄ⲛ ⲟⲩⲛⲉ̄ⲋ ⲧⲁⲣ ⲕⲉⲗⲗⲓ ⲇⲁ̄ⲣⲓ̄.
Guwwal goon uneeh tar kelli daarii.
Even an ant has a mind according to its size.

[Advice not to underestimate anyone, even they may think differently.]

---

1 A Nubian waterwheel doesn't have blades, but hoppers (baked earthenware jars).

(8)

ⲥⲉⲅⲉⲇ ⲛⲁⲃⲃⲉⲇⲓⲕⲁⲛ ⲁⲣⲁⲫⲁⲱⲓ ⲙⲓⲛⲅⲁ ⲁ̄ⲱⲓ?
Seged naccecikan arafaawii minnga aawii?
What does a Rifaie[2] do after a scorpion sting?

> [Advice that help is better before or during a problem, not after it has passed.]

(9)

ⲉⲅⲉⲇⲧⲁ ⲫⲁ̄ⲅⲓⲗ ⲟⲩϣⲓⲕⲕⲁⲛ ⲙⲓⲛⲅⲁ ⲁ̄ⲱⲓ?
Egedta faagil ushikkan minnga aawii?
What hurts the sheep, if you hit it on its fur?

> [Used when someone has nothing to lose.]

(10)

ⲅⲟⲇⲇⲟ ⲅⲟ̄ⲩⲛⲓⲕⲕⲁ ⲅⲓⲛⲇⲓ ϣⲁⲕⲕⲟⲩⲙⲟⲩⲛ.
Goddo guunyikka gindi shakkumun.
Thorns will not befall those who look at where they place their feet.

> [Be careful before doing anything.]

(11)

ⲅⲓⲛⲇⲓ ⲇⲁ̄ⲅⲓ ⲫⲉⲛⲧⲓ ⲕⲁⲙⲙⲟⲩⲛ.
Gindi jaagi fenti kammun.
Whoever is afraid of thorns will not eat dates.

> [To those who want to get something, yet fear the troubles that may come.]

---

2   The Rifaie Sufi group is known for their ability to control snakes and scorpions.

(12)

Ⲧⲟⲩⲅ ⲅⲓⲧⲧⲓⲅ ⲙⲉ̄ⲛⲕⲁⲛ ⲥⲓⲅⲓⲣ Ⲧⲁⲯⲯⲓⲙⲟⲩⲛ.
Tuug gitting meenkan sigir tanynyimun.
If the wind is not strong, the boat will not sail.

[If you want to do something, you must prepare well and wait for the appropriate conditions.]

(13)

Ⲫⲓⲗⲁ̄ⲛ ⲙⲁ̄ⲯⲓⲛ Ⲧⲟ̄ⲩ ⲅⲁⲗⲁⲅⲁ.
Filaan maanyin tuu galaga.
Someone who is precious as the eyeball.

[Said about dear friends.]

(14)

Ⲫⲓⲗⲁ̄ⲛ ⲟⲣⲣⲉ̄ Ⲧⲟ̄ⲩ Ⲧⲁⲛⲛⲁ Ⲛⲉϳⲓⲙⲟⲩⲛⲛⲁ.
Filaan orree tuu tanna neyimunna.
Someone cannot water a pea in his stomach.

[Said about someone who cannot keep a secret.]

(15)

Ⲫⲓⲗⲁ̄ⲛ ϫⲟⲩⲛⲧⲓ ⲥⲟⲩⲧⲣⲟⲩⲙⲟⲩⲛ.
Filaan junti sutrumun.
Someone doesn't hide the pregnant woman.

[Said to encourage keeping secrets.]

(16)

ⲫⲓⲗⲁⲅⲟⲩ ⲙⲟⲩⲣⲧⲓ ⲅⲟ̄ⲛ ⲱⲓⲥⲗⲁⲅⲅⲓ ⲅⲟ̄ⲛ ⲁⲗⲁⲅⲁ ⲙⲉⲛⲛⲁ.
Filaangu murti goon wislangngi goon alaga menna.
People who act like a horse and a snake.

> [Said about those who always disagree with each other in any discussion or situation.]

(17)

ⲫⲓⲗⲁ̄ⲛ ⲧⲁ̄ⲅⲓⲁ ⲧⲁⲛⲛⲁ ⲟⲩⲙⲙⲟⲩⲛⲛⲁ.
Filaan taagya tanna ummunna.
Someone who wears a skullcap not his size.

> [Said about someone who is arrogant.]

(18)

ⲫⲓⲗⲁ̄ⲛ ⲇⲓ̄ⲥ ⳝⲉⳝⲉⲗ ⲟⲩⲣⲟⲩⲙ ⲁⲗⲁⲅⲁ.
Filaan diis jebel urum alaga.
Someone whose blood is as thick as a black mountain.

> [Said about someone who is boring, stodgy, or dreary.]

(19)

ⲫⲓⲗⲁ̄ⲛ ⲇⲓⲣⳝⲁⲇⲓⲛ ⲟ̄ⲓ̄ⲅⲁ ⲕⲁⳝⲁⲫⲓ.
Filaan dirbadin ooyga kabafi.
Someone who ate a chicken leg.

> [Said about someone who walks a lot without purpose.]

(20)

ⲫⲓⲗⲁ̄ⲛ ⲇⲓⲣⳝⲁⲇ ⲕⲟⲩⲙⳝⲟⲩ ⲕⲁ̄ⲅⲓ ⲛⲁⲕⲓⲧⲧⲁⲛ ⲇⲁⲱⲱⲓⲗ ⲇⲁ̄ⲫⲓ.
Filaan dirbad kumbu kaagi nakittan dawwil daafi.
Someone like a chicken that has an egg that does not stop moving.

> [Said about someone who walks a lot without purpose.]

(21)

ⲇoyⲛⲧi ⲗā̄ⲅiⲛ/ⲁj̈ ā̄ⲅⲣi̅ⲛ ⲱō oyⲛoyⲥⲕⲁⲣ.
Junti laagin woo unuskar/ay aagriin woo unuskar.
The pregnant person is/I am sitting, oh nurse!

[Said to someone who does something that other people are supposed to do.]

(22)

ⲧi̅ ⲇā̄ⲛⲙoyⲛ ⲙiⲗⲗi̅ ⲅⲁ ⲙiⲗⲗiⲛⲛⲁ.
Tii jaanmun millii ga millinna.
Before buying the cow, they prepare the rope/shackle.

[Said about someone who builds castles in the air.]

(23)

ⲧiⲛo ⲗā̄ⲅiⲛ ⲙⲁⲧⲧoⲛ ⳉⲁⲃⲁⲣⲕ ⲉⲇⲛⲁ.
Tino laagin matton habark edna.
In the west he wants to know the news of the east.

[Said about someone who gets the news from others without leaving their place.]

(24)

ⲱē̄ⲕō̄yⲛ ⲧiⲗiⲧⲁ j̈iⲙⲙⲉⲛi̅ ⲧⲁⲕⲕⲁ ā̄ⲅ ⲫⲉⲇⲇiⲣoyⲛ ⲱⲁⲅⲧiⲛ ⲇōyⲣē̄.
Weekuun tilita yimmenii takka aag feddirun wagtin juuree.
We wasted time, while urging him to get the job done.

[Said about someone who is too lazy to do what is required of them.]

(25)

ⲧⲟⲩⲃⲁⲣⲣⲁ ⲅⲓⲗⲗⲓⲓⲧⲓ ⲃⲓⲛⲓⲛⲛⲁ.
Tuubarra gilliitii biininna.
Upon crossing the waters, the male sex organs appear.

> [Said about a situation that tests someone's merit.]

(26)

ⲓⲇⲉⲛ ⲟⲩⲕⲕⲓ ⲛⲉⲇⲁ.
Ideen ukki neeja.
Woman's ears do not hear.

> [Said when gossip is spoken behind someone's back.]

(27)

ⲇⲟⲩⲛⲧⲓⲗ ⲧⲟⲩⲗ ⲇⲁⲫⲓⲕⲕⲟⲛⲛⲓⲙ ⲓⲣⲃⲉ.
Juntil tuul daafikoonnim irbee.
He knows what a pregnant woman has inside.

> [Said about someone who claims to know all hidden secrets.]

(28)

ⲫⲁⲓⲁ ⲅⲉⲣⲓⲓⲗⲗⲉ ⲫⲉⲅⲓⲣⲁ?
Faaya geryillee fegiira?
Is someone who writes and reads a teacher?

> [Said about someone who claims to be knowledgable.]

(29)

ⲟⲩⲥⲟⲩⲣ ⲱⲓⲣⲇⲁⲫⲓⲛ ⲃⲁⲗⲗⲁⲩⲁ ⲕⲁⲥⲁⲕⲁⲅⲓ.
Usur wirjafiin balaanya kaasakaagi.
Turban on the head but his ass is bare.

> [Said about someone who should be doing something that's more important than he's doing now.]

(30)

ⲁⲇⲉⲙ ⲇⲟⲩϣ ϩⲁⲧⲁⲃⲁⲛ ⲕⲓⲇⲓⲗ ⲙⲁⲣⲣⲁ ⲛⲟⲩⲱⲱⲟⲅ ⲟⲩϣⲉ̄ⲛ.
Aadem doosh hataban kidil marra nuwwog usheen.
Only an idiot hits the threshold twice.

[Said about those who do not learn from their previous mistakes and keep making them.]

(31)

ⲧⲁⲗⲗⲉ ⲅⲟ̄ⲛⲓⲙ ⲕⲓⲗⲓⲅ̄ⲅⲓ ⲧⲓⲣⲓⲥⲥⲁ ϳⲓⲙⲉⲛⲓ.
Talle goonim kilingngi tirissa yimeni.
Even a needle when it falls it sounds like iron.

[Advice not to underestimate the details.]

(32)

ⲉⲇⲇⲓⲅ ⲟⲩⲥⲟ̄ⲩ̄ⲣⲣ ⲟⲩⲇⲓⲙⲙⲉ̄ⲛⲕⲁⲛ ϣⲟⲅⲟⲗⲙⲟⲩ.
Eddig usuurr udimmeenkan shogolmu.
He is like scissors, you have move him with your fingers.

[Said about someone who does nothing without being moved by others.]

(33)

ⲉⲇⲇⲓⲅ ⲕⲁ̄ⲅⲓⲅ̄ⲁ ⲟⲩⲥⲟⲩⲣⲣⲁ ϣⲁⲕⲕⲓⲛ.
Eddig kaaginga usurra shakkin.
He puts what is in his hand in his ass.

[Said when someone miscalculates or lacks knowledge of what he owns.]

(34)

ⲕⲁϬⲓⲛ ⲫⲁⲗⲁⲗ ϩⲉⲣⲣ ⲟⲇⲉ̄.
Kabin falal jerr odee.
He pees in the pot that he eats from.
Cast no dirt into the well that gives you water.

> [Said about ungrateful people.]

(35)

ⲅⲟⲩⲱⲱⲁⲗ ⲧⲟ̄ⲛ ⲥⲟ̄ⲩ ⲇⲁⲕⲕⲓⲛ.
Guwwal toon suu dakkin.
He milks the ant.

> [Said about someone who takes thing to their limit.]

(36)

ⲙⲁ̄ⲇⲉⲗ ⲱⲟ̄ Ϭⲟⲩⲇⲟ̄ⲩⲣⲓⲛ ⲯⲉⲡⲕⲁ ⲙⲟⲩⲣⲧⲓ ⲛⲟ̄ⲩϬⲕⲁⲛ ⲕⲁⲋⲋⲁ ⲧⲟ̄ⲩⲗ ⲧⲟⲩⲕⲕⲓⲛⲁⲛ.
Maadel woo buduurin shepka murti nuubkan kacca tuul tukkinan.
What a pity, if the horse falters, they will hit the donkey.

> [Said about someone who bullies the weak.]

(37)

ⲛⲁⲣ ⲧⲁⲛⲅⲁ ⲙⲟⲩⲣⲧⲟⲩⲙⲟ̄ⲩⲛⲓ ⲁϊ ⲧⲁⲛⲅⲁ ⲙⲟⲩⲣⲧⲟⲩⲙⲟⲩⲛ.
Nar tannga murtumuuni ay tannga murtumun.
He who does not control his tongue does not control himself.

> [Said to encourage keeping secrets.]

(38)

ⲕⲁⲇⲓⲛ ⲛⲓⲱϫⲓ Ⲫⲉϫⲓⲕⲁⲛ.
Kajin niishii feyikan.
When the donkey grows horns.

[Said about things that are impossible.]

(39)

ⲕⲁⲃⲁⲅⲟⲛ ⲙⲓⲣⲧⲓ ⲇⲁⲅⲁⲍⲓⲅⲟⲛ ⲁⲅⲁⲣ ⲧⲁⲛⲛⲁ ⲟⲩⲇⲓⲣ.
Kabagoon mirti jagahigoon agar tanna udir.
Take a part of the bread and put it back complete.

[Said about things that are impossible.]

(40)

ⲅⲉϫ ⲗⲟⲕⲕⲁ ⲍⲓⲕⲟⲛ ⲁⲙⲁⲛⲅⲁ ⲧⲉⲛⲁⲛⲁ.
Gey lokka hiikoon amannga teenana.
Even if someone is on a raft you give him water.

[Advice about doing the right thing.]

(41)

ⲟⲯⲓⲛ ⲕⲟ ⲗⲟⲯⲕⲁⲛ ⲛⲓⲙ ⲟⲯⲁ ⲧⲟⲟⲓⲛⲛⲁ.
Onyin koo lonykan nim onya toocinna.
When the family of the dead person cries we can cry with them.

[Advice to take care of your own business first before you ask others to help.]

(42)

ⲕⲁⲃⲁ ⲟⲩⲧⲧⲟⲩ ⲛⲁϫⲓⲕⲕⲁⲛ ⲕⲉⲣⳃⲁ ⲅⲟ̄ⲛ ⲛⲉ̄ ⲟⲩⲧⲧⲟⲩ ⲛⲁ̄?
Kaba uttu nayikkan kersha goon nee uttu naa?
If food belongs to people, does your stomach also belong to them?

> [Said about an insatiable person who eats the food of others excessively; take care of yourself and eat slowly.]

(43)

ⲕⲟ̄ⲥⲟ̄ⲥⲓ ⲉⲗⲗⲓ ⲥⲟⲩⲃⲁ ⲕⲁⲥⲥⲁ ⲇⲁ̄ϩⲙⲟⲩⲛⲛⲁ.
Koosoosi eddi suba kassa daajmunna.
The person who is satisfied does not lick their fingers.

> [Advice that when someone is content they will not ask for more.]

(44)

ⲇⲓⲫⲫⲓⲛ ⲟⲣⲟ ⲥⲟ̄ⲩⲣⲓ̄ⲇ ⲱⲁⲗⲁ̄ ⲇⲓⲫⲫⲓⲛ ⲕⲁⲗⲟ ⲥⲟ̄ⲩⲣⲓ̄ⲇ.
Diffin oro suuriid walaa diffin kalo suuriid.
Neither South Castle broth nor North Castle broth.

> [Said about someone who didn't get what they had hoped for.]

(45)

ⲁⲣϫⲉ̄ ϩⲟⲩⲅⲣⲁ ⲓⲛⲓⲛ ⲓⲙⲓ̄ⲇⲧⲁ ⲇⲟⲩⲙⲙⲓⲛ.
Arjee jugra inin imiidta dummin.
You add salt to *arjee*[3] while it's boiling.

> [Advice to do the right thing at the right time.]

---

3   *Arjee* is a Nubian dish.

(46)

ⲇⲟⲅⲉ̄ⲛ ⲟⲩⲣⲣⲁ ⲅⲟ̄ⲛ ⲱⲉ̄ ⲇⲁ̄ⲣⲓ ⲧⲁⲕⲕⲁ ⲃⲓⲅⲓⲇⲓⲗ ⲗⲁⲅⲟ̄ⲛ ⲱⲉ̄ ⲇⲁ̄ⲣⲓ.
Dogeen urra goon wee daari takka bigidil lagoon wee daari.
The dove thinks one thing and the hunter something else.

[Said when there's a diversity of views or interests.]

(47)

ⲁ̄ⲇⲓ ⲇⲟⲩⲱⲱⲁⲅⲅⲟ̄ⲕⲁⲛ ⲙⲟⲩⲅⲣⲓ̄ⲛ ⲃⲁⲧⲁⲣⲁⲅⲅⲟ̄ⲛⲁ.
Aadi duwwangngookan mugriin batarangngoona.
When the hyena gets old, it becomes a mockery of dogs.

[Said when someone of former power or influence loses their position.]

(48)

ⲁⲥⲥⲁⲣⲓ̄ⲛ ϫⲉⲗⲗⲓ ⲉⲇⲇⲓⲅ ⲟⲣⲕⲓⲕⲕⲁⲛⲅⲟ̄ⲛ ⲁⲓ̈ⲅⲁ ⲟⲣⲕⲟⲩⲙⲙⲟⲩⲛ.
Assariin jelli eddig orkikkangoon ayga orkummun.
Your children's work at house or in the field may comfort your hands, but not your heart.

[One should not be dependent on the work of others (especially children) and do their own work by themself.]

(49)

ⲫⲉⲗⲉ̄ⲛ ⲅⲁⲧⲧⲓ ⲟⲩⲱⲱⲟ ⲓ̈ⲙⲙⲟⲩⲛⲛⲁ.
Feleen gatti uwwo yimmunna.
An onion doesn't have two smells.

[Said against double standards.]

(50)

ⲚⲀⲖⲔⲞⲨⲘⲘⲞ̄ⲨⲚ ⲚⲀⲖⲦⲒ ⲄⲀ̄ⲤⲒ̈ⲎⲀ̄.
Nalkummuun nalti gaasiyaa.
It's hard to see when you haven't seen.

> [Said when poor people suddenly become rich and openly flaunt it.]

(51)

ⲀⲖⲒ̄ ⲦⲀ ⲀⲖⲒ̄ⲖⲒⲚ.
Alii ta aliilin.
Ali will be Ali.

> [Said about someone who does not change.]

(52)

ⲀⲚⳠⲒ ⲦⲀⲰⲰⲞ ⲦⲀⲄⲄⲀ ⲚⲞⲨⲢⲔⲒⲘⲞⲨⲚ.
Anbi tawwo tangnga nurkimun.
The dum palm[4] doesn't shade what's underneath.

> [Said when someones does something for the benefit of strangers, rather than their own family.]

(53)

ⲞⲨⳠⲞⲨⲢⲦⲒ ⲀⲘⲀⲄⲀ ⲔⲞⲘⳠⲞ̄ ⲔⲒⲘⲘⲞⲨⲚ.
Uburti amanga komboo kimmun.
Ash does not overburden the water.

> [Those who collect their money in crooked ways do not benefit from it.]

---

4 *Hyphaene thebaica.*

(54)

ⲁⲗⲁⲇ ⲁϳ ⲧⲁⲛⲅⲁ ⲕⲁϳⲙⲟⲩⲛ.
Alad ay tannga kaaymun.
The ax does not fix itself.

> [Said about someone who benefits or advises others, but not himself.]

(55)

ⲅⲁⲣⲣⲓ ⲅⲟ̄ⲩ ⲗⲉ̄ ⳗⲉⲃ̄ⲉⲕⲁ ⲗⲟⲅ ⳝⲟ̄ⲩⲕⲉⲥⲥⲁ?
Garri guu lee shebeeka log guukessa?
Is it possible that the bad guys go to the shrine of Sheikh Shebika?[5]

> [Said when someone see a thief or punk next to a mosque or the shrine of a saint.]

(56)

ⲁⲃ̄ⲁⲅ ⲟⲩⲛⲛⲁ ⲕⲟⲩⲧⲧⲓⲗⲟⲛ ⳗⲁ̄ϳ ⲙⲉ̄ⲛⲁ.
Abaag unna kuttilon waay meena.
Flies will not fly after our departure.

> [Said by someone who is leaving as a curse to those who he is leaving behind that nothing will happen after his departure.]

(57)

ⲧⲁⲣ ⲕⲟ̄ ⲛⲁⲇⲇⲓ ⲟⳣⳣⲙⲟⲩⲛ.
Tar koo naddi onynymun.
The one who falls by himself does not cry.

> [Said about someone who caused self-harm and is then fed up with it.]

---

5   Sheikh Shebika was a righteous and pious man and a saint.

(58)

Ⲃⲁⲍⲁⲣ ⲟⲩⲗⲟⲩⲙ ⲕⲓⲯⲯⲓⲗ ⲍⲟⲩⲥⲥⲁⲛ ⲕⲟϭ.
Bahar ulum kinynyil hussan koc.
Swim freely in a river without crocodiles.

> [Said to advise a person to seize the opportunity in the absence of those who may deter him, or as a mockery of seizing opportunities in an unethical manner.]

(59)

Ⲁⲙⲁⲛ ⲉⲗⲗⲓ ⲧⲁⲛⲛⲁ ⲧⲟ̄ⲛ ⲛⲁⲗⲗⲟⲩⲙⲟⲩⲛ.
Aman eddi tanna toon naddumun.
The water does not drip between his fingers.

> [Said about an extremely miserly person.]

(60)

Ⲇⲁ̄ⲙⲟⲩⲛ ⲕⲓϭϭⲁⲇ ⲍⲉ̄ⲣⲕⲁ ⲇⲟⲗⲗⲟⲙⲟⲩⲛ.
Daamun kiccad heerka dollomun.
A deer who grew up in deprivation did not like good things.

> [Said about someone used to a bad situation who cannot adjust to a good situation.]

(61)

Ⲁⲱⲣⲓⲕⲕⲓ ⲱ̆ⲁ̄ⲣⲧⲓⲛ ⲧⲁⲱⲱⲟ ⲫⲓ̄.
Ashrikki shaartin tawwo fii.
Beauty lies under the spears.

> [Protect honor and decent manners, if necessary by sword.]

(62)

ⲀⲘⲀⲚ ⲪⲀⲖⲀⲒ̄ⲈⲖ ⲔⲒⲆⲆⲒ.
Aman faalayeel kiddi.
To sink into a bowl of water.

[Said about someone who cannot deal even with small tasks.]

(63)

ⲘⲀ̄Ⲩ ⲤⲞ̄ⲨⲆ ⲔⲒⲚⲚⲀⲆⲦⲀ ⲆⲞⲨⲘⲘⲞⲘⲞⲨⲚ.
Maany suud kiccadta dummomun.
The eye does not catch/hunt deer by itself.

[Said to encourage hard work.]

(64)

ⲦⲈ̄ⲖⲀⲪⲒ̄Ⲛ ⲪⲀⲲⲒⲔⲒⲢⲞ̄ⲔⲀⲚ ⲄⲈⲚⲀ.
Teelafiin fashikirookan gena.
It's better to get it done while it's hot.

[Said to encourage doing work on time and not delaying it.]

(65)

ⲔⲞⲨⲦⲦⲒ ⲤⲞⲢⲞⲄ ⲦⲀⲚⲚⲀ ⲞⲔⲔⲞⲘⲞⲨⲚ.
Kutti sorong tanna okkomun.
Flies do not fall on his nose.

[Said about the arrogant people.]

(66)

ⲅⲁⲗⲃⲁ̄ⲛ ⲕⲁⲃⲁ ⲇⲉ̄ⲱⲓⲗ ⲕⲁⲣϫ̑ⲙⲟⲩⲛ.
Galbaan kaba deewil karjmun.
A poor man's bread is not baked on a baking plate.[6]

> [Advice that when a poor person speaks, no one listens to him because of their poverty.]

(67)

ⲱⲓⲣⲓⲕⲕⲁⲛⲇⲓ ⲇⲧⲇⲉ̄ ⲱⲁⲗⲗⲟⲩⲙⲟⲩⲛ ⲱⲁⲗⲗⲓⲕⲁⲛⲅ̄ⲟ̄ⲛ ⲕⲁⲣϫ̑ⲙⲟⲩⲛ.
Shirikkandi diidee wallumun wallikangoon karjmun.
The cooking pot of partnership doesn't boil, and when it's boiled it's not cooked well.

> [Advice that it is better to do things on your own rather than have two people in charge.]

(68)

ⲁⲙⲁⲛ ϫ̑ⲁⲃⲁⲇ ⲗⲟⲅ ⲇⲁⲣⲣⲓ.
Aman jabad log darri.
Water rises through the shallow place.

> [Advice that you have to do things step by step, in their right order.]

(69)

ⲥⲉⲣⲓ̄ⲩ ⲙⲁⲣⲣⲁ ⲅⲟⲣϫ̑ⲟ ⲅⲁⲣⲃⲓⲕⲁⲛⲅ̄ⲟ̄ⲛ ⲓⲗⲗⲉ̄ⲅ̄ⲙⲟⲩⲛ.
Seriiny marra gorjo garbikangoon illeengmun.
Barley will not become wheat, even if it is sifted six times.

> [Said about someone who has a trait that will never change.]

---

6 A *deew* is a Nubian baking plate made of clay on which bread is baked over a fire.

(70)

ⲕⲟⲩⲗⲕⲁ ⲫⲓⲛⲇⲓ ⲕⲟⲩⲗ ⲧⲁⲛⲛⲁ ⲧⲟ̄ⲣⲓ
Kulka findi kul tanna toori.
Whoever digs a hole falls in it.

[Said when someone intended to harm others, but only harms themself.]

(71)

ⲧⲁⲧⲧⲟ̄ⲩⲣⲓⲛ ⳝⲟⲩ ⲱⲉ̄ ⲇⲓ̄ⲇⲉ̄ ⲫⲓⲣⲣⲁⲫⲓ̄ⲕⲁ ⲛⲁⲣⲣⲁⲕⲉ̄
Tattuurin ju wee diidee firrafiika narrakee.
One root of a bitter apple[7] makes the whole bowl bitter.

[Advice that you have to pay attention to detail, one wrong step can make an entire effort go to waste.]

(72)

ⲁⲩϣⲓⲇⲇⲁⲛ ⲕⲓⲣⲟ ⲧⲟⲩⲅⲟⲩⲣⲓⲇⲇⲁⲛ ⳝⲟⲩ.
Ashiddan kiro tuguriddan ju.
Come with the placenta, go with the shroud.

[Said about the difficulty of changing a person's characteristic that accompanies them until their death.]

(73)

ⲧⲟ̄ⲩⳡⲓⲛ ⲛⲟ̄ⲅⲓⲗ ⲅⲁⲗⲁⲃⲁ ⲓⲥⲕⲓⲧⲧⲁ.
Tuungin noogil galaba iskitta.
In a house of boys, poverty is a guest.

[The poverty of a family that has many male children does not last long.]

---

7 Also known as colocynth.

(74)

ⲕⲟⲩⲧⲧⲁ ⲙⲉⲛⲇⲁ ⲱⲓⲣⳜⲉ ⲗⲉⲕⲓⲛ ⲁ̄ⲅⲓⲛⲧⲁ̄ⲛ ⲱⲓⲣⳜⲓⲕⲁⲛ ⲅⲉⲛⲁ.
Kutta menja wirje lekin aagintaan wirjikan gena.
It's better to undress while you are sitting than while standing up.

> [Said when someone loudly announces their plan but then ultimately fails. It is better to be modest and only proclaim success when you're done.]

(75)

ⲟⲩⲛⲛⲓⲥⲁⲛ ⲧⲟⲅⲟⲗ ⲁ̄ⲅⲓ.
Unnisan togol aagi.
He is still in the place (terrace) where he was born.

> [Said about someone who does not develop with time, someone ignorant who has done nothing in their life.]

(76)

ⲟⲩⲧⲧⲟ̄ⲩⲛ ⲧⲟ̄Ⳝ ⲁⲙⲁ̄ⲛⲅⲁ ⲕⲟⲩⲙⲙⲟⲩⲛⲛⲁ.
Uttuun tood amaannga kummunna.
You cannot count on other people's children.

> [Advice to rely on your own family.]

(77)

ⲟⲩⲣⲧⲓ ⲕⲟⲩⳌⲉ̄ ⲧⲁⲛⲛⲁ ⲧⲟ̄ⲛ ⲫⲁⲗⲓⲕⲕⲁ Ⳝⲉⲗⲉⲅ ⲕⲁⳄⲓ.
Urti kudee tanna toon falikka jeleg kabi.
The sheep that are far from the fold are eaten by the wolf.

[Said about someone who disturbs his family and offends them.]

(78)

ⲟⲩⲫⲫⲓ ⲫⲓⲗⲗⲓⲗ ⲫⲓⲛⲇⲓ ⲫⲓⲗⲗⲓ ⲧⲟ̄ⲣⲓ.
Uffi fillil findi filli toori.
The crooked wedge fits into the crooked hole.

[Said about a notorious woman marrying a similar man.]

(79)

ⲟⲩⲗⲟⲩⲙⲙⲁ ⲇⲟⲩⲙⲙⲓ ⲟⲩⲗⲟⲩⲙⲙⲁ ⲅⲁ̄ⲣⲓ.
Ulumma dummi ulumma gaari.
When the crocodile tries to prey upon you, embrace it.

[Said about someone who is compelled by circumstances to submit to others for fear of their retribution.]

(80)

ⲙⲟⲩⲅ ϫⲉⲗⲉⲱ ⲧⲁⲅⲅⲁ ⲁϭⲟⲩⲙⲟⲩⲛ.
Mug jelew tangnga acumun.
A dog does not bite its tail.

[Said about someone who favors their family and protects them from any harm.]

(81)

ⲕⲁ̄ⲥⲓⲣⲕⲁ ⲕⲁ̄ⲥⲓ ⲙⲁⲗⲗⲉ̄ ⲓⲇⲁⲓ̈ⲙⲙⲟⲩⲛ.
kaasirka kaasi mallee idayimmun.
Not all turban wearers are men.

[Said when someone boast they are able to do something, but then are unable to do so.]

(82)

ογττογΝ ελλι λοΓ καΔι κōcмογΝ.
Uttun eddi log kabi koosmun.
He who eats with the hand of others will not be satisfied.

[Said to encourage people to rely on themselves.]

(83)

ΓαψψιρκΔ ογψιρ мēΝκαΝ Διc ψαρмογΝ.
Ganynyirka ushir meenkan diis warmun.
Blood does not flow without razors or weapons.

[Advice that you have to start if you want to finish.]

(84)

Διϳōcι τογΓορκα мāρмογΝ.
Diyoosi tugorka maarmun.
He who dies will find a shroud.

[Goodness will prevail, and if a person is poor or weak, they will find someone to save them from their predicament.]

(85)

ΔιϳολατōΝ τογΓογρκα ΔογκκI.
Diyolatoon tugurka dukki.
He takes off the shroud from the dead.

[Said about someone sneaky who does anything to get what they want.]

(86)

ⲉⲗⲗⲓ ⲱⲉ̄ ⲇⲉⲣⲕⲁ ⲇⲉⲗⲉⲱⲙⲟⲩⲛ.
Eddi wee jerka jelewmun.
We can not wash our back with one hand.

[Said to encourage cooperation and engagement with others.]

(87)

ⲅⲁⲣⲃ̄ⲁⲛ ⲙⲁⲩⲁⲕⲕⲁ ⲙ̄ⲣⲙⲟⲩⲛ.
Garbaan mashakka miirmun.
A sieve does not block the sun.

[It is impossible to hide facts, especially for those trying to hide something with lies.]

(88)

ⲉⲗⲗⲓ ⲙⲁⲩⲁⲕⲕⲁ ⲧⲓⲅⲓⲣⲙⲟⲩⲛ.
Eddi mashakka tigirmun.
A hand does not cover the sun.

[Said about someone who commits themself to things beyond their ability.]

(89)

ⲙⲁⲣⲇⲁⲛ ⲇⲓⲫⲫⲓ ⲅⲟⲩⲇⲁⲅⲟⲩⲙⲟⲩⲛ.
Marjan diffi gonydangumun.
A fortress of lies cannot be built.

[Said to encourage not lying. If you lie once, people may believe you, but if you keep lying, people will one day know that you are a liar.]

(90)

ⲅⲟⲩⲥⲥⲉ̄ ⲧⲁⲕⲕⲁ Ⲫⲟⲕⲟⲕⲕⲁ ⲓⲣⲃ̄ⲉ.
Gussee takka fokokka irbee.
The silo knows who opened it.

> [Two meanings: everyone knows their own advantages and disadvantages; a girl/woman knows who took her virginity.]

(91)

ⲟⲩϣⲓ̄ⲉⲱⲣⲉⲇⲁ ⲕⲓⲣ ⲧⲁⲕⲕⲁ ⲕⲟ̄ⲅ ⲧⲉ.
Oshshii ewreda kir takka koog te.
The servant sows and gives to his master.

> [Said when all of someone's efforts only benefit somebody else instead of themself.]

(92)

ⲯⲓⲃⲓⲣ ⲟⲩⲕⲕⲓ ⲕⲓⲛⲯⲓⲛ ⲥⲟⲕⲕⲓⲇⲁⲕ ⲕⲟⲩⲙⲟⲩⲛ.
Shibir ukki kinyin sokkidak kumun.
The basket is not lifted without its handles.

> [The right path is the right way to do things.]

(93)

ⲓⲇⲉ̄ⲛ ⲇⲉ̄ⲱⲓⲛ ⲯⲁ̄ⲗⲁ ϩⲓⲇ̄ⲇⲁⲅ ⲙⲁ̄ⲣⲓⲙⲙⲟⲩⲛ.
Ideen deewin shaala hijjag maarimmun.
A woman will not lack reason in the kitchen.

> [Advice that the kitchen is a woman's domain.]

(94)

ⲕⲁⲃⲁⲕⲕⲁ Ⲫⲉⲧⲓⲱⲱⲕⲁⲛ ⲕⲁⲱⲱⲓ Ⲫⲓ.
Kabakka fetishshkan kashshi fi.
If you look carefully at the bread, you find straw.

[Advice not the keep looking for mistakes because you'll always find something that's wrong.]

(95)

ⲥⲉⲥⲥⲟⲩⲣ ⲱⲁⲓⲁⲪⲓⲗⲗⲁⲧⲟⲛ ⲱⲓⲅⲓⲣⲧⲓⲅ Ⲃⲓⲱⲱⲓ.
Sessuur waayafiillatoon shingirtig bishshi.
He can pluck the feathers of a bird while flying.

[Said about someone with speedy hands/work and good luck.]

(96)

ⲁⲇⲉⲙ ⲛⲟⲅⲓⲗⲧⲟⲛ Ⲫⲁⲕⲕⲁⲛ ⲉⲣⲣⲁⲓⲕⲁⲅⲟⲛ ⲧⲁⲃⲁⲅⲓ.
Aadem noogiltoon fakkan errayikkangoon tabagi.
If a person leaves his home, he encounters many things, good or bad.

[Life is to move, stagnation is death.]

(97)

Ⲫⲉⲛⲧⲓ ⲧⲁⲱⲱⲟ ⲧⲁⲛⲛⲁ ⲁⲅⲓⲛ ⲛⲁ.
Fenti tawwo tanna aagin na.
The beneficiary of the palm is for who sitting beneath it.

[Those close by benefit while those far away will be deprived.]

(98)

ⲦⲞⲨ ⲒⲔⲔⲀ ⲘⲞⲚⲒ ⲒⲔⲔⲀ ⲆⲞⲖⲖⲒⲘⲞⲨⲚ.
Tuu ikka mooni ikka dollimun.
The heart that hates you will not love you.

[Your enemy will not change their feelings toward you.]

(99)

ⲄⲒⲒ ⲆⲞⲨⲦⲦⲒⲄ ⲆⲞⲢⲀ ⲆⲞⲨⲘⲘⲞ.
Gii juttig jora dummo.
The maternal uncle swore that this is his nephew and took him.

[Said when you have to trust someone on their word.]

(100)

ⲔⲞⲨⲖⲔⲀ ⲪⲒⲚⲆⲒⲔⲀⲚ ⲈⲤⲔⲒⲒⲆⲒⲚ ⲄⲈⲢ ⲪⲀⲖⲘⲞⲨⲚ.
Kulka findikan eskiidin geer falmun.
If you dig a hole, you only get dirt.

[Said to people if they quarrel with the intention to reconcile them and persuade them to start a new page.]

(101)

ⲞⲨⲦⲦⲞⲨⲚ ⲈⲆⲆⲒ ⲀⲘⲀⲚ ⲆⲈⲢⲀ.
Uttun eddi aman jera.
The hands of people are behind the river.

[Help is far away.]

(102)

ⲒⲢⲒⲒⲚ ⲔⲀⲂⲈⲚ ⲔⲞⲒ ⲆⲈⲤⲤⲀ.
Iriin kaben koy dessa.
The tree that you eat is green.

[A metaphor for a happy life.]

(103)

ⲫⲟⲩⲇⲉ̄ⲛ ⲃ̄ⲁⲃⲟⲩ ⲅⲟ̄ⲛ ⲫⲁ̄ⲃⲃⲁ ⲕⲟⲩⲛⲓ.
Fuudeen baabu goon faabba kuni.
Also the ladybug has a father.

[Said about those who talk about the pride of their ancestor.]

(104)

ⲟⲩⲣⲟⲩⲙ ⲗⲁ̄ⲕⲓ̄ⲛ ⲙⲁⲗⲗⲓ ⲅⲉⲛⲁ.
Urum laakiin malli gena.
Browne is better than black.

[Said when choosing between multiple things.]

(105)

ⲙⲟⲣⲉ̄ ⲕⲓϭϭⲁⲇⲧⲁ ⲇⲟⲩⲙⲙⲓⲙⲟⲩⲛ.
Moree kiccadta dummimun.
The acacia tree[8] will not satiate deers.

[Said when food and clothing are not enough.]

(106)

ⲙⲁⲣⲕⲁⲧⲧⲓⲛ ⲁ̈ⲓ ⲇⲟⲩⲕⲕⲁⲫⲓ.
Markattin ay dukkafi.
A thief's heart is terrified.

[Said when someone makes a mistake and is afraid of a reprimand.]

---

8 *Acacia ehrenbergiana* Hayne.

(107)

ⲦⲞⲆ ⲒⲔⲔⲀ ⲪⲈⲚⲚⲒ ⲰⲈⲆⲒⲀⲦⲞⲚ ⲂⲒⲚⲒ.
Tood ikka fenni weediltoon biini.
A child who benefits their family shows this in the cradle.

> [Said to a family or group member in order to criticize the bad behavior of a child or other group member.]

(108)

ⲒⲔⲔⲀ ⲆⲞⲀⲀⲒ ⲤⲈⲢⲔⲀ ⲄⲞⲀⲀⲀⲦⲈ.
Ikka dolli seerka gollate.
He who loves you swallows pebbles for you.

> [Said when someone tolerates and accepts the actions of their loved ones.]

(109)

ⲚⲞⲢ ⲒⲔⲔⲀ ⲦⲈⲚⲀⲄⲀ ⲪⲒⲢⲄⲒⲔⲀⲚ ⲚⲈⲢⲀⲪⲒⲚⲄⲞⲚ ⲦⲈ.
Noor ikka teenanga firgikan neerafiingoon te.
If God wants good for you, he may give it to you while you are asleep.

> [Said when someone finds good luck.]

(110)

ⲘⲞⲨⲢ ⲄⲒⲚⲆⲒⲄ ⲞⲨⲚⲚⲒⲘⲞⲨⲚ.
Muur gindig unnimun.
A tamarisk tree does not bear thorns.

> [Said in order to defend a good person from accusations, or advice that people will not change their nature, whether it is good or bad.]

(111)

ογκκι ογςκο̄ν ογκκε̄ν ΜαςκοΝ ογκκε.
Ukki uuskoon ukkeen maskoon ukkeen.
The ear that hears bad things also hears good.

[Life has good and evil.]

(112)

ιΔε̄Ν ο̄ⳝςκα ιΔε̄Ν Νογ τογκκ.
Ideen uuska ideen nog tukk.
It takes a woman to hit a bad woman.

[Advice not to interfere into women's quarrels.]

(113)

Γοδιρκα κο̄ϳ̈ ταΝΝογ ολλε̄Να.
Gojirka kooy tannog olleena.
The carcass is hanged from its foot.

[One has to do things in their proper place/time.]

(114)

Δο̄ⲯ, Δο̄ⲯ αϳ̈Γα κο̄Γ ιρϐε̄ρ.
Doony, doony ayga koog irbeer.
Raise me as you want, eventually I will know my family.

[Advice not to rely too much on people outside your group/family.]

(115)

ⲕⲁⲙ ⲕⲟⲣⲟⲩ ⲧⲁⲛⲛⲟⲅ ⲕⲓⲯⲯⲓⲙⲟⲩⲛ.
Kam korony tannog kinynyimun.
The camel does not get tired of carrying a hump.

> [One does not get tired of the thing that benefits them, no matter how difficult it is.]

(116)

ⲁⲥⲥⲁⲣⲓⲛ ⲫⲁⲩⲩⲉⲕⲕⲁ ⲧⲁⲛⲛⲉ̄ⲛ ⲟⲩⲙⲉ̄ⲛⲕⲁⲛ ⲓⲣⲃⲟⲩⲙⲙⲟⲩⲛ.
Assarin fanynyekka tanneen onymeenkan irbummun.
When they cry, a mother knows that her baby is hungry.

> [Advice that you have to be explicit about your needs in order for other people to understand them and to help you.]

(117)

ⲅⲟⲩⲧⲧⲓⲛ ⲧⲟ̄ⲩⲗ ⳝⲁⲕⲕⲁⲣⲕⲁ ⲟⲗⲗⲉ̄.
Guttin tuul jakkarka ollee.
Throwing the fishing rod inside the jar.

> [Said about someone who puts something out of place or asks for something at an inappropriate moment.]

(118)

ⲟⲩⲕⲕⲓ ⲟⲩⲕⲕⲓⲛ ⲇⲟ̄ⲣⲟ ⲕⲉϳⲓⲙⲟⲩⲛ.
Ukki ukkin dooro keyimun.
One ear will not be larger than the other

> [Said about those who flaunt their family and friends.]

(119)

ⲧⲟⲅⲟⲇⲓⲛ ⲕⲓⲇⲓⲁ ⲧⲟ̄ⲣⲟ.
Togojin kidil tooro.
He flew with a slingshot stone.

[Said about some who left their home and never returned, with no hope of finding them.]

(120)

ⲅⲓⲣⲓⲇ ⲟⲩⲥⲟⲩⲣ ⲧⲁⲛⲅⲁ ⲛⲁⲗⲕⲟⲕⲕⲁⲛ ⳓⲁ ⲁⲣⲁⲅ ⲕⲟⲩⲙⲙⲟⲩⲛ.
Girid usur tannga nalkokkan fa arag kummun.
If the monkey saw own his anus he wouldn't dance.

[Said of someone who does not see their own faults and criticizes other people.]

(121)

ⲁⲅⲓⲥⲥⲓ ⲕⲟ̄ⲥⲕⲁⲛ ⳓⲁⲧⲧⲁ ⲛⲁⲇⲇⲓ.
Angissi kooskan fatta naddi.
If a fish is satisfied, it jumps onto the shore.

[Advice to someone who has recently become rich and flaunts his wealth.]

(122)

ⲓⲇⲉ̄ⲛⲓⲛ ⲇⲟⲡⲡⲉ̄ ⲓ̄ⲅⲓⲛ ⲁⲅⲁⲣⲣⲁ ⲇⲟⲡⲡⲓ.
Ideenin jorree iigin agarra jorri.
He pees in the place where his wife asks him to do.

[Said about a man who is subjugated by his wife.]

(123)

ⲧⲁⲯⲯⲁⲧⲧⲓ ⲧⲁⲃⲁⲅⲁⲧⲧⲓ.
Tanynyatti tapagatti.
Much walk much dirty.

> [Said about a person who walks without purpose/benefit.]

(124)

ⲉⲅⲉⲇ ⲃⲉⲅⲁⲧⲧⲓ ⲇⲁⲛ ⲧⲁⲯⲯⲓ ⲃⲉⲅⲁⲧⲧⲁ.
Eged beengatti dan tanynyi beengatta.
Whoever accompanies the bleating sheep becomes like her.

> [Said when those who are similar in behavior accompany each other.]

(125)

ⲁⲥⲕⲁⲣⲕⲁ ⲙⲟ̄ⲩⲥⲉ ⲓ̄ⲅⲥⲁⲛⲇⲟ ⲟⲩⲕⲕⲓⲣ ⲕⲟⲩⲙⲙⲟⲩⲛ.
Askarka Muuse iigsando ukkir kummun.
We have not heard of this since they called the soldier Moses.

> [Said when referring to a rare thing or event.]

(126)

ⲁⲃⲓⲗⲉⲥⲉ̄ⲛ ⲛⲟⲅ ⲇⲓⲣⲃⲁⲇⲧⲁ ⲱⲁ̄ϳⲓⲅⲉⲛⲛⲁ?
Abileseen nog dirbadta wayingenna?
Does the fox guard the chicken?

> [Said to encourage finding the right people for the right job.]

(127)

ⲯⲟ̄ⲣⲧⲓⲅ ⲟⲩⲇⲣⲟⲛ ⲅⲉ̄ⲣ ⲟ̄ⲥⲙⲟⲩⲛ.
Shoortig udron geer oosmun.
Only he who created your soul (life) can take it.

> [Said to encourage someone to face their fear or say the truth.]

(128)

ⲙⲁⲣⲕⲁⲧⲧⲓ ⲅⲟⲩⲥⲥⲉ̄ⲛ ⲱ̑ⲁ̄ⲇⲟ ⲍⲓ͠ⲇⲇⲁⲅ ⲙⲁ̄ⲣⲓⲙⲙⲟⲩⲛ.
Markatti gusseen shaado hijjag maarimmun.
A thief always has a reason to be in front of the granary.

[Said about the someone guilty when they try to exonerate themself.]

(129)

ⲧⲟ̄ⲩ ⲓⲛⲛⲓⲛ ⲉⲛⲛⲁ ⲕⲟⲩⲙⲙⲉ̄ⲛⲉⲕⲕⲁ ⲟⲩⲧⲧⲟ̄ⲩⲛ ⲧⲟ̄ⲩ ⲉⲛⲛⲓⲙⲟⲩⲛ.
Tuu innin enna kummeenekka uttuun tuu ennimun.
The secret that you could not keep in your chest, surely others cannot.

[Advice about keeping the secrets hidden.]

(130)

ⲁ̄ⲇⲉⲙ ⲇⲉⲣ ⲧⲁⲛⲅⲁ ⲛⲁⲙⲙⲟⲩⲛ.
Aadem jer tannga nammun.
A person does not see his back.

[Advice that you always need others, no one can just live by themselves.]

(131)

ⲥⲉⲅⲉⲇⲓⲛ ⲕⲁⲃⲥⲓ̄ⲛ ⲫⲟ̄ⲩⲇⲉ̄ⲅ ⲇⲁ̄ⲅⲓ.
Segedin kabsiin fuudeeg jaagi.
Someone bitten by scorpion fears beetles.

[Said when avoiding a specific activity because of a previous bad experience.]

(132)

oypin ⲙⲟ̄ⲛⲉⲕⲕⲁ ocⲙⲁp ⲗⲟⲅ coⲕⲕ.
Urin moonekka osmar log sokk.
Put the load your head doesn't like on your shoulder.

> [Advice about sharing and dividing responsibilities.]

(133)

ⲁ̄ⲧⲉ̄ⲗ ⲁ̄ⲅⲓ ⲓⲕⲕⲁ ⲕⲁⲙⲙⲟyⲛⲛⲁ ⲱⲟ̄ ⲓⲗⲗⲉ̄.
Aateel aagi ikka kamunna woo illee.
Someone who sits in the shade does not eat you, oh wheat!

> [Advice that you will not benefit unless you put in the work.]

(134)

oⲱⲱⲁ̄ ⲙⲟ̄pⲕⲁ ⲇⲟ̄ⲅⲇⲁ ⲙⲁ̄ⲱⲉ̄ ⲱⲉ̄ⲗⲁ ⲕⲓⲇⲇⲟⲛ.
Oshshaa moorka joogja maassee weela kiddon.
After the maid ground an artab[9] of wheat, she drowned in a quarter[10] of keleh.

> [Said about someone who is successful in major matters but incapacitated by a minor incident.]

(135)

ceyyⲁ ceyⲟⲛⲛⲁ ⲱⲁⲗⲗⲁ ⲅⲁⲃⲇⲟⲛⲛⲁ.
Seyya seyonna walla gabdonna.
What about the money? Is it for the one who saved it or the one who took it?

> [Said to the miser who only hoards money rather than enjoying it.]

---

9 About 50 kg.
10 About 0.562 kg.

(136)

ⲛⲁⲡⲓⲛ ⲕⲟ̄ⲅⲟ̄ⲛ ⲫⲁⲇⲇⲁⲛ ⲕⲟ̄ⲇⲟ ⲥⲁⲣⲙⲓ.
Napin koogoon faddan koodo sarmi.
Who owns gold needs who owns silver.

[People need each other to live.]

(137)

ⲙⲉⲣⲅⲁⲣ ⲧⲁⲛ ⲕⲟⲩⲥⲁⲫⲓ̄ⲛ ⲧⲁⲣⲓ̄ⲛ ␀ⲁⲯⲯⲉ ⲙⲓⲛⲁ?!
Mergar tan kusafiin tariin banynye mina?!
What is he saying, and his pants are loose?!

[Said about someone who reproaches other people while forgetting his own shortcomings.]

(138)

ⲁ̄ⲇⲓ ⲛⲟ̄ⲅ ⲧⲁⲅⲅⲁ ␀ⲁ̄ⲅⲙⲟⲩⲛ.
Aadi noog tangnga jaagmun.
A hyena is not afraid of his home.

[A person lives as he is used to.]

(139)

ⲧⲁⲧⲧⲟ̄ⲩⲣ ⲛⲁⲕⲓⲣ ⲱⲁ̄ⲇⲟ ⲁ̄ⲣⲓ.
Tattuur nakir shaado aari.
He looks like a bitter apple[11] crawling out.

[Said about someone who always looks to benefit from others.]

---

11 Also called colocynth. This refers to the way in which the bitter apple plant grows.

(140)

oyTTōyN KITTāN coKKΔ ΔoyMM.
Uttuun kittaan sokka dumm.
It's borrowed clothes, so make sure not to get dirty.

>[Said about someone who boasts with borrowed things or shows off in front of people, thinking that they do not know the truth.]

(141)

ΓΔρῙϐIN ōjΓΔ KOρKOTTIΔ TIΓINNΔ.
Gariibin ooyga korkottil tiginna.
He traces the feet of strangers on dry clay.

>[Said when someone is doing something useless or superfluous, or about someone who is too curious.]

(142)

cῙw ōyc ΔρKI ōycKΔ kāρI.
Siiw uus arki uuska kaari.
Bad sand is looking for bad clay.

>[Like attracts like.]

(143)

TEMEN TῙN ΓēwΓΔ ΓōȳѰIN NEKIN ΓOρONΔI INNIN ΓOρMāѰѰΔ ΓōȳѰKΔN ΓENΔ.
Temen tiin geewga guunyin nekin gorondi innin gormanynya guunykan gena.
It is better to look at your bull's testicles than to look at your neighbor's cow udder.

>[Advice on how to be content.]

(144)

ⲁⲂⲟⲅ ⲓⲇ ⲱⲉ̄ⲣⲁϳ ⲇⲁ̄ⲣⲁ ⲙⲟⲩⲅ ⲁ̄ⲅ ⲱⲟⲕⲕⲓ.
Aboog id weeray daara mug aag wokki.
The dog thought my father a stranger and barked at him.

[Said when something is contrary to reality.]

(145)

ⲥⲓⲅⲓⲡ ⲟⲩⲧⲧⲓ ⲧⲁⲛⲛⲁ ⲇⲉⲅⲓ.
Sigir utti tanna degi.
Each boat is moored to anchor.

[Things should be in their proper place.]

(146)

ⲥⲉⲣⲓ̄ⲩ ⲁϳ ⲧⲁⲛⲅⲁ ⲥⲟⲕⲕⲉⲇⲁ ⲛⲉ̄ ⲓⲟ̂ⲓⲕⲕⲁ ⳝⲁ ⲥⲟⲕⲕⲓ.
Seriiny ay tangnga sokkeda lee iccikka fa sokki.
Does barley carry itself? To carry others.

[Said when asking someone to do something that they cannot do for themself.]

(147)

ⲇⲓϳⲁ ⲇⲟ̄ⲣⲟ ⲧⲟⲣⲂⲁⲅ ⲙⲁ̄ⲣⲓⲙⲙⲟⲩⲛ.
Diya jooro torbag maarimmun.
The dead will not lack a grave.

[Said about someone who definitely will find help from the benevolent.]

(148)

ⲆⲒⲣⲂⲀⲆⲒⲚ ⲞⲒ̈ⲅⲀ ⲔⲀⲂⲀⲎⲒ.
Dirbadin ooyga kabahi.
As he ate a chicken leg.

> [For the person who walking a lot without purpose.]

(149)

ⲅⲞⲨⲰⲰⲀⲣⲒ̄Ⲛ ⲅⲈⲘⲒⲚ ⲎⲞ̄ⲖⲔⲀ ⲆⲞ̄ⲖⲈⲔⲔⲀ ⲔⲀⲘⲒⲚ ⲞⲒ̈ ⲰⲈ̄ ⲈⲚⲚⲈⲞ̄Ⲟ̄Ⲁ ⲚⲞⲅⲒ.
Guwwariin gemin hoolka doolekka kamin ooy wee ennecca nogi.
What ants collected in a year, the camel scattered with a kick.

> [Said about the inability of the weak to resist injustice.]

(150)

ⲦⲒⲂⲒⲤⲤⲒ̄Ⲛ ⳍⲀⲔⲔⲒⲀ ⲦⲀⲖⲖⲈ̄ ⲘⲒⲚⳍⲀ Ⲁ̄ⲰⲒ̄.
Tibissiin fakkil tallee minnga aawii.
What can a needle do among iron studs?

> [Said about someone weak who thinks that they can overthrow the powerful.]

(151)

ⲂⲈⲚⲀ̄ⲦⲒ̄ ⲞⲔⲔⲈ̄ ⲘⲀⲖⲖⲈ̄ ⲒⲆⲈ̄ⲚⲀ ⲒⲘⲘⲞⲨⲚ.
Benaatii okkee mallee ideena yimmun.
Not everyone wearing a scarf is a woman.

> [Appearances are deceiving.]

(152)

Ⲁ̄ⲆⲒⲚ ⲚⲞ̄ⲅⲒⲀ ⲅⲒⲤⲒⲣ ⲂⲀ̄ⲒⲘⲞⲨⲚ.
Aadin noogil gicir baaymun.
The house of a hyena always has bones.

> [Said about a rich person denying they have money.]

(153)

ⲇⲉⲗⲗⲓ Ⲇⲓϳⲓⲕⲕⲁ ⲙⲁ̄ⲩ ⲇⲁ̄ⲅⲓ.
jelli diyikka maany jaagi.
The eye is afraid of too much work.

> [Said to encourage starting to work and finish the assigned tasks.]

(154)

ⲕⲁⲙ ⲙⲉⲥⲕⲟ̄ⲕⲁⲛ Ⲇⲉⲅⲉⲣ ⲦⲀⲚⲄ̄ⲞⲚ ⲉⲥⲕⲁ ⲥⲟⲕⲕⲟⲙⲟⲩⲛ.
Kam meskookan deger tanngoon eska sokkomun.
If a camel gets old, it is unable to carry its saddle.

> [Advice to assign work or responsibility according to ability.]

(155)

ⲦⲀⲂⲒⲆⲒⲚ ⲦⲞ̄Ⲇ ⲄⲀⲢⲢⲒ ⳬⲞⲄⲄⲀ ⲦⲀⲚⲚⲀⲦⲞ̄Ⲛ ⲪⲀⲗⲓ.
Tabidin tood garri shogga tannatoon fali.
The unfortunate blacksmith's son lost his clothes.[12]

> [Said when a person brought evil from where he expected goodness.]

(156)

ⲁ̄Ⲇⲓ ⲦⲀⲢⲒⲚ ⲔⲞ̄ⳞⲒⲚ ⲀⲄⲀⲢⲢⲀ ⲦⲞ̄Ⲛ Ⲃⲁ̄ϳⲙⲟⲩⲚ.
Aadi tarin koosin agarra toon baaymun.
A hyena does not leave the place where he is satisfied.

> [Said about someone if they repeatedly go to a place where they always finds something good (e.g., fishing or hunting spot).]

---

12 Blacksmiths used to roam the villages of Nubia and provide services to people throughout the year for no charge, and then received their wages at the end of the season from the harvest (wheat and barley). It is reported that one of these blacksmiths went to a farmer to take the part of the harvest he was due, as they used to. The farmer asked him to give him his clothes to bring the grain, the blacksmith gave him his clothes, and the farmer left and did not return.

(157)

ⲙⲁⲣⲧⲓⲛ ⲕⲟⲩⲃ̄ⲃⲓⲕⲕⲁ ⲗⲉⲅⲉⲛⲓⲛ ⲕⲟⲩⲃ̄ⲃⲓⲕⲕ ⲁⲗⲁⲅⲁ ⲕⲓⲣⲟⲛ.
Martin kuccikka legenin kuccikk alaga kiron.
He is bathing in a canal as if he's bathing in washtub.

> [Said about someone who is acting recklessly, or in order to remind someone of their former poverty.]

(158)

ⲥⲁⲗⲃⲟ ⲟⲩⲫⲫⲓ ⲁⲙⲁⲛⲅⲁ ⲇⲟⲩⲙⲓⲙⲟⲩⲛ.
Salbo uffi amannga dumimun.
The leaky waterbag does not hold water.

> [Said to a someone who is wasting a lot of money, to encourage saving.]

(159)

ⲕⲁⲃⲁⲛ ⲉⲇⲇⲓ ⲛⲁⲥⲥⲓⲣⲁ.
Kaban eddi nassira.
The hand that eats is long.

> [Said about a guest if their host points to some food and tries to bring it closer to them.]

(160)

ⲟ̄ⲓ̈ ⲓⲛⲛⲓ ⲓⲕⲕⲁ ⲇⲟⲗⲗⲓⲛ ⲁⲅⲁⲣⲣⲁ ⲅⲟ̄ⲛ ⲉⲇ̄ⲇⲟⲩ ⲙⲟ̄ⲛⲓⲛ ⲁⲅⲁⲣⲣⲁ ⲅⲟ̄ⲛ ⲉⲇ̄ⲇⲟⲩ.
Ooy inni ikka dollin agarra goon ejju moonin agarra goon ejju.
Your feet lead you to the place you love and the place you hate.

> [Your decisions and choices are yours.]

(161)

ⲕⲁⲇⲓⲥ ⲩⲓⲃⲃⲁ ⲙⲉⲥⲕⲁ ⲓⲫⲫⲧ ⲓⲓⲟⲛ.
Kadiis shibba meska iffii iyon.
The cat, unable to reach the food, said it was disgusted.

> [Said about a person who requests something but when they are unable to get it, reduce its value.]

(162)

ⲕⲁⲇⲓⲥ ⲩⲓⲃⲃⲁ ⲙⲉⲥⲕⲁ ⲥⲟⲩⲛ ⲕⲓⲣⲣⲓⲧⲁ ⲓⲓⲟⲛ.
Kadiis shibba meska suun kirriita iyon.
The cat, unable to reach the food, said it was only buttermilk.

> [Said about a person who requests something but when they are unable to get it, reduces its value.]

(163)

ⲅⲟⲩⲣⲕⲁ ⲇⲁⲅⲓⲕⲕⲁ ⲅⲟⲩⲣ ⲫⲁⲗⲁⲧⲉ.
Gurka jaagikka gur falate.
What you are afraid of you find.

[Advice concerning unduly magnifying your fear of something.]

(164)

ⲥⲓⲱ ⲓⲇⲇⲟ ⲱⲉⲣⲓ.
Siiw iddo weeri.
To cultivate in barren sand.

> [Said about a wasted effort, or those who do useless work.]

(165)

ⲇⲁⲕⲓⲅⲟⲩⲗⲟⲛ ⲃⲁⲣⲣⲓⲗ ⲃⲁⲓ̈ⲙⲉⲛⲁ.
Jaakiguulon barril baaymeena.
May fearful things not be absent from the place.

>[Advice that fear is necessary in order for people to act well.]

(166)

ⲁⲇⲟⲱⲱⲓⲛⲅⲟⲛ ⲥⲁⲍⲓⲃⲓⲛ ⲁⲅⲓⲗⲗⲟⲅ ⲧⲟⲣⲓ.
Adowwingoon saahibin agillog toori.
Your enemy may reach you through your friend's mouth.

>[Advice about the importance of keeping secrets.]

(167)

ⲅⲟⲩⲥⲥⲉⲛ ⲧⲟⲩⲛ ⲉⲇⲁⲛⲁ.
Gusseen tuun edaana.
A call to prayer inside a grain silo.

>[Said about someone who speaks and advises, but no one listens or follows their advice.]

(168)

ⲥⲁⲙⲉ ⲧⲓⲅⲓⲣⲉⲇⲁ ⲁⲣⲁⲅⲓ.
Saamee tigireda aragi.
He hides his beard and dances.

>[Said about someone who does something that contradicts their venerable appearance.]

(169)

ⲛⲟ̄ⲣⲓⲛ ⲙⲁ̄ⲥⲓⲛ ⲅⲓⲛⲇⲉ̄ⲛ ⲟⲩⲕⲕⲓ ⲱⲉ̄ ⲛⲁⲇⲇⲓⲙⲟⲩⲛ.
Noorin maasin gindeen ukki wee naddimun.
The thorn does fall only by the will of God.

[Said about God's almighty hand ruling the universe.]

(170)

ⲕⲁⲇⲓⲛ ⲇⲓϳⲉ ⲙⲟⲩⲅⲣⲓ̄ⲛ ⲃⲁⲗⲉ̄.
Kajin diye mugriin balee.
The donkey dies, the dogs rejoice.

[Said about someone who benefits from the misfortunes of others.]

(171)

ⲕⲓⲧⲧⲓ ⲫⲁ̄ⲣⲇⲓⲕⲁⲛ ⲙⲟⲩⲅⲓⲛ ⲱⲟⲕⲕⲓⲕⲁⲛⲅ̄ⲟ̄ⲛ ⲟⲣⲣⲓ.
Kitti faarjikan mugin wokkikangoon orri.
Shabby clothes tear even from dogs barking.

[Said as a consolation for the loss of a loved one, also to warn against pessimism and to show that everything has a life span.]

(172)

ⲛⲓ̄ⲇ ⲟⲩⲱⲱⲟⲛ ⲫⲁⲕⲕⲓⲗⲧⲟ̄ⲛ ⲫⲁⲗⲟ̄ⲥϳⲓ ⲇⲓⲫⲫⲓ ⲕⲟⲗⲟⲧⲧⲁ ⲁⲧⲧⲓ.
Niid uwwon fakkiltoon faloosyi diffi kolotta atti.
What comes out of your teeth (words) will be heard in seven castles.

[Said about the importance of keeping secrets and the speed that news and rumors spread.]

(173)

ⲉⲱⲣⲟ ⲗⲓⲙ ⲅⲟ̄ⲣⲓ ⲱⲟ̄ ⲓⲗⲗⲉ̄ⲛ ⲅⲁⳟⲁⲣⲉ.
Ewro lim goori woo illeen gangare.
Only the one who sows reaps you, oh seeds of wheat.

[Advice about putting in the work to achieve results.]

(174)

ϣⲓⲃⲓⲣⲓⲛ ⲟⲩⲫⲫⲓⲗⲟⲅ ⲛⲁⲇⲇⲟ̄ⲥⲟⲛ.
Shibirin uffilog naddooson.
He fell from the bottom of the basket.

[Said about someone who is ignored, marginalized, or underestimated.]

(175)

ⲫⲁⲧⲓ̄ⲥⲁⲛ ⲕⲟ̄ ⲫⲁⲧⲓ̄ⲥⲁⲛ ⲅⲁⲧⲧⲓⲅ ⲥⲟⲩⲛⲛⲟⲩⲙⲟⲩⲛ.
Fatiisan koo fatiisan gattig sunnumun.
The owner of an animal's rotting corpse is not harmed by its smell.

[Said about someone who is in shock from sudden loss and does not appear to act appropriately.]

(176)

ⲇⲟⲩⲱⲱⲓⲣⲓ̄ⲛ ⲛⲁⲱⲁ ⲕⲁⲙⲓⲛ ⲕⲟⲛⲕⲁⲗⲉ̄ⲗⲟⲅ ⲟⲩϣⲓⲣⲕⲁⲛⳟⲟ̄ⲛ ⲫⲟⲧⲧⲁ ⲫⲁⲗⲓ.
Duwwiriin nawa kamin konkaleelog ushirkangoon fotta fali.
If you hit the elderly's skin with camel dung it falls off.

[Said about human weakness in old age.]

(177)

ⲓⲛⲇⲟⲛ ⲟ̄ⲩⲥⲓ ⲛⲟ̄ⲡⲓⲛ ⲛⲟ̄ⲅⲓⲗⲅⲟ̄ⲛ ⲟ̄ⲩⲥⲁ.
Indon uusi noorin noogilgoon uusa.
Who is bad here is also bad in the house of God.

[The good are good and the wicked are wicked everywhere.]

(178)

ⲕⲁϭϭⲁ ⲇⲟ̄ⲅⲁⲫⲓ ⲟ̄ϳⲗⲟⲅ ⲇⲁⲣⲓⲛ ⳅⲓⲥⲁ̄ⲡⲡⲁ ⲁ̄ⲱⲙⲟⲩⲛ.
Kacca doogafi ooylog daarin hisaappa aawmun.
Who rides a donkey does not care about who walks on their feet.

[Said about the rich not caring about the poor.]

(179)

ⲅⲟⲣⲟⲛⲇⲓⲛ ⲉⲱⲱⲣⲉ ⲅⲟⲣⲟⲛⲇⲓⲛ ⲟⲩⲥⲟⲩⲣⲣⲁ ⲇⲁ̄ⲫⲓ.
Gorondin ewwre gorondin usurra daafi.
What the bull sows is in the bull's ass.

[Said about someone who only benefits themself.]

(180)

ϳⲁ̄ ⲕⲁⲇ ⲇⲓϳⲟⲛ ϳⲁ̄ ⲕⲁϭϭⲁ ⲱⲉ̄ⲅⲓ ⲇⲓϳⲟⲛ.
Yaa kaj diyon yaa kacca weegi diyon.
Either the donkey dies or the one who leads it dies.

[Said about the boredom of a long wait.]

(181)

ⲕⲁⲇ ⲥⲓⲇⲇⲟ ⲙⲟⲣⲙⲟⲕⲓ? ⲟ̄ⲩⲃⲟⲩⲣⲧⲓⲛ ⲇⲟⲩⲕⲕⲓⲇⲁ.
Kaj siddo mormoki? uuburtin dukkila.
Where does the donkey roll? Where the ash is.

[Said about people or things that can always be found in the same spot.]

(182)

ⲟⲩⲧⲧⲟ̄ⲩⲛ ⲧⲉ̄ⲗⲟⲛ ⲓⲕⲕⲁ ⲉⲛⲛⲓⲕⲁⲛⲅⲟ̄ⲛ ⲟⲩⲧⲧⲟ̄ⲩⲛ ⲛⲟ̄ⲅ ⲓⲕⲕⲁ ⲉⲛⲛⲟⲩⲙⲟⲩ.
Uttuun teelon ikka ennikangoon uttuun noog ikka ennumu.
If the graveyard of others takes you, their house does not.

> [Advice not to intrude on others.]

(183)

ⲃⲟⲩⲣⲟⲩⲅ ⲉⲇⲙⲟⲩⲛ ⲁⲅⲟⲅ/ⲉ̄ⲛⲅ ⲉⲇ.
Burug edmun agog/eenng ed.
Marry the mother-in-law/mother, not her daughter.

> [Advice to choose a good spouse by looking at their mother-in-law, because the future spouse will look like them.]

(184)

ⲓⲥⲕⲓⲛⲧⲉ̄ ⲇⲓⲅⲓⲇ ⲕⲟⲩⲗⲕⲁ ⲫⲓⲛⲇⲓⲙⲟⲩⲛ.
Iskintee digid kulka findimun.
Many mice don't dig a hole.

> [Advice about the distribution of tasks at work, because too many people involved may be unproductive.]

(185)

ⲕⲁⲛⲇⲓ ⲛⲟ̄ⲅ ⲧⲁⲛⲅⲁ ⲓⲣⲃⲉ̄.
Kandi noog tannga irbee.
The knife knows its sheath.

> [Said about someone who insists on their opinion without caring about the others opinion, or who takes a path that others see as improper.]

(186)

ⲕⲟⲩⲧⲧⲁ ⲙⲉⲛⲇⲁ ⲱⲓⲣⲇⲓⲗⲉⲕⲓⲛ ⲁ̄ⲅⲓⲛⲧⲁ̄ⲛ ⲱⲓⲣⲇⲓⲕⲁⲛ ⲅⲉⲛⲁ.
Kutta menja wirjilekin aagintaan wirjikan gena.
Undressing while sitting is better than undressing standing.

> [Said about someone who exposes himself more than his abilities allow and reveals his modest abilities.]

(187)

ⲕⲁⲙ ⲕⲟⲣⲟⲩ̄ ⲧⲁⲛⲅⲁ ⲅⲟ̄ⲩⲩ̄ⲙⲟ̄ⲩ̄ⲛ ⲓ̄ⲟ̄ⲟ̄ⲓ ⲕⲟ̄ⲩⲛⲓ ⲛⲁⲗⲓ.
Kam korony tannga guunymuun icci kuuni nali.
A camel sees the hump of the others but does not see its own.

> [Said about someone who does not see their own sins while talking about those of others.]

(188)

ⲥⲓⲅⲓⲣⲕⲁ ⲕⲁ̄ⲓ̄ⲧⲟⲧⲧⲓ ⲧⲁⲛⲛⲁ ⲇⲉⲅⲉ̄.
Sigirka kaayii otti tanna degee.
He who made a boat places it in its anchor/place.

> [Said about things or speaking in the right place or time.]

(189)

ⲱⲓⲇⲇⲁ ⲧⲓⲣⲧⲓ ⲙⲁ̄ⲩ̄ⲩ̄ⲁ ⲙⲉⲣⲓⲛ.
Widda tirti maanynya merin.
Gifts and charity prevent envy.

> [Advice about giving gifts and *zakat*/charity.]

(190)

ⲉⲇⲇⲓ ⲁⲛⲛⲓ ⲇⲓ̂ⲇⲁ ⲕⲉⲃ̂ⲃ̂ⲁⲇ ⲱⲉ̄ⲕⲟ̄ⲛ ⲟⲕⲕⲁⲫⲓ̄ⲛ.
Eddi anni dija keccaad weekkoon okkafiin.
He has five fingers, plus another one.

[Said about someone who has to take care of himself, and carry out his work on his own.]

(191)

ⲱⲓ̄ⲥⲕⲓⲇⲓⲛ ⲅⲟⲩⲥⲥⲉ̄ ⲥⲟ̄ⲩⲇⲁ.
Wiiskidin gussee suuda.
The container of debt is empty.

[Advice to discourage borrowing.]

(192)

ⲱⲟⲕⲕⲁⲧⲧⲓⲛ ⲙⲟ̄ⲗⲗⲁ ⲧⲓ̄ⲅⲓ ⲱⲟⲕⲕⲁⲧⲧⲁ.
Wokkattin moola tiigi wokkatta.
Whoever lives next to the one who barks becomes the same.

[Advice to choose your friends carefully.]

(193)

ⲉⲇⲇⲓ ⲁⲛⲛⲟⲅ ⲙⲁ̄ⲩ ⲁⲛⲅⲁ ⲇⲟⲩⲕⲕⲓⲥ.
Eddi annog maany annga dukkis.
With my hand I hurt my eyes.

[Said about someone who harms himself without intention.]

(194)

ⲟⲩⲧⲧⲟ̄ⲩⲛ ⲉⲇⲇⲓⲗⲟⲅ ⲕⲁⲃⲓ ⲥⲓⲅⲁⲫⲓ.
Uttuun eddilog kabi sigafi.
Food will get stuck in the throat of he who eats with the hand of others.

[Advice to get the job done by yourself.]

(195)

ⲅⲁⲩⲯⲓⲣⲕ ⲟⲩⲯⲓⲣ ⲙⲉ̄ⲛⲕⲁⲛ ⲇⲓ̄ⲥ ⲱⲁⲣⲙⲟⲩⲛ.
Ganynyirk ushir meenkan diis warmun.
Blood does not flow without razors or a weapon.

[Tasks will be accomplished by starting work.]

(196)

ⲁⲫⲓⲗⲗⲁⲧⲟ̄ⲛ ⲛⲉ̄ ⲧⲟⲩⲫⲫⲁ ⳝⲁ̄ⲙⲉ̄ ⲕⲟⲩⲥⲙⲟⲩⲱⲁ?
Agillatoon nee tuffa shaamee kusmuwa?
Do we wipe our beard by spitting on it?

[Said about someone who insults themself or their family by disgraceful work.]

(197)

ⲁⲅⲓⲗⲗⲁⲧⲟ̄ⲛ ⲧⲟⲩⲫⲫⲁ ⲥⲁ̄ⲙⲉ̄ⲗ ⲟⲩⲇⲓⲙⲟⲩⲛⲛⲁ.
Agillatoon tuffa saameel udimunna.
When we spit, we do not spit on our beard.

[Advice to someone who insults themself or their family to stop doing so.]

(198)

Ⲇⲓⲟⲕⲟⲩⲛⲁⲛ ⲕⲟⲛⲛⲁ Ⲇⲁⲫⲫⲓ.
Diyokuunaan koonna daaffii.
He is in the world of the dead.

> [Said when referring to a useless person.]

(199)

Ⲓⲧⲧⲓⲣⲕⲁ ⲟⲕⲕⲉ̄ Ⲧⲁⲫⲫⲁ Ⲇⲁϩⲓ.
Ittirka okkee taffa daaji.
He who cooks ittir[13] tastes it.

> [Advice to be certain of the quality of your work before you show it to others, or be certain of your own benefit when working for others.]

(200)

ⲉⲆⲆⲓ ⲱⲉ̄ ϩⲉⲣⲕⲁ ϩⲉⲗⲉⲱⲙⲟⲩⲛ.
Eddi wee jerka jelewmun.
You cannot wash your back with one hand.

> [Advice that one needs to cooperate with others in life.]

(201)

ⲔⲟⲗⲉⲆ Ⲧⲁⲕⲕⲁ Ⲓⲣⲃⲟⲩⲙⲟⲩⲛⲓⲛ ⲟⲩⲥⲟⲩⲣⲕⲁ ϩⲟⲩⲅⲉ.
koled takka irbumunin usurka juge.
The one who does not know the smoke pit will burn her ass.[14]

> [Advice not to ignore the advice of people with specialized knowledge.]

---

13 *Ittir* is a popular Nubian dish, cooked from mallow or fennel, coriander, and dried okra powder.
14 The story of the proverb is that a Nubian woman perfumes her husband who returns from traveling by placing perfume and incense in a pit and sitting naked on top of it wrapped in a thick cover in what looks like a sauna to imbue her body, and the woman who is ignorant of how this custom and craftsmanship burns her ass.

(202)

ⲍⲁ̄ⲇⲁ Ⲇⲁ̄ⲣⲓ ⲟ̄ⲩⲥⲕⲁ ⲕⲟⲩⲙⲙⲟⲩⲛ.
Haaja daari uuska kummun.
The things we have will not be bad.

[Advice not to underestimate anything, even simple, you may need it in the future.]

(203)

Ⲅⲓⲣⲓⲇ ⲁⲃⲁⲗⲁ̄ⲡ ⲓⲇⲇⲁⲛ ⲧⲁⲡⲡⲓ.
Girid abalaany iddan tanynyi.
A monkey accompanies monkeys.

[Said about someone who looks like those who accompany them.]

(204)

Ⲫⲟ̄ⲩⲇⲉ̄ ⲧⲁⲛⲛⲁⲥⲕⲁ ⲗⲟ̄ⲩⲗⲁ ⲓ̄ⲅⲓⲛ.
Fuudee tannaska luula iigin.
The beetle calls her daughter a pearl.

[Parents love their children, they see them as the greatest in the universe.]

(205)

Ⲙⲓⲣⲥⲁ̄ⲗ ⲍⲓ̃ⲇⲇⲓⲅ ⲍⲓ̃ⲇⲇⲓⲙⲟⲩⲛ.
Mirsaal hijjig hijjimun.
Your messenger does not perform the Hajj for you.

[Said about someone who asks others to do their work instead of doing it by themself.]

(206)

ārmoynin tī goronδir oynni.
Aagmunin tii gorondig unni.
The absent person's cow gives birth to a bull.[15]

> [Said to encourage someone to do their job well.]

(207)

cirip koycaɸī maλλēλa δappi.
Sigir kusafii malleela darri.
He sails with every boat.

> [Said about a weak personality or opportunist.]

(208)

δawwiλog δāpikka rinδē ɯakkmoyn.
Dawwilog daarikka gindee shakkmun.
Thorns won't harm who walks on known roads.

> [Advice that someone who deviates from their path will be harmed.]

(209)

āδem δaгaδтa ɸeλēn oykki ɯē δere.
Aadem jagadta feleen ukki wee dege.
A weak person can be tied with onion leaves.

> [Said about an unimportant person.]

---

15 Cows are more beneficial to the rural than the bulls because they give birth and their newborn can be sold in addition to their milk.

(210)

ⲅⲟⲣⲟⲛⲇⲓ ⲟⲩⲱⲱⲟ ⲕⲟⲩⲇⲉⲗ ⲇⲁⲣⲙⲟⲩⲛ.
Gorondi uwwo kudeel darmun.
Two bulls are not tied at the same place.

[Said when there are too many bosses at work.]

(211)

ⲥⲓⲅⲓⲣⲕⲁ ⲕⲟⲩⲙⲙⲟⲩⲛⲓ ⲥⲓⲅⲓⲣⲓⲛ ⲫⲓⲛⲇⲉ̄ⲓ̈ⲁ.
Sigirka kummuni sigirin findeeya.
If you do not have a boat, be a dock.

[Advice to work with what you have and within your means.]

(212)

ⲧⲉⲙⲉⲛ ⲛⲉ̄ⲣⲕⲁⲛ ⲛⲓⲙ ⲛⲉ̄ⲣⲓⲛⲛⲁ.
Temen neerkan nim neerinna.
Sleeping after checking the sleep of the neighbors.

[If a neighbor suffers from a problem, there is no rest or sleep until we help him solve it.]

(213)

ⲇⲓ̄ⲇⲉ̄ ⲟⲩⲥⲟⲩⲣ ⲧⲁⲛⲛⲟⲅ ⲧⲉ̄ⲗⲓ.
diidee usur tannog teeli.
The pot heats from the bottom to the top.

[Said to encourage someone to take the proper measures to reach the goal, and it is often said to criticize someone who uses wrong methods to reach their goal.]

(214)

ⲧⲟ̄ⲩ̄ⲅ ⲇⲟⲩⲕⲕⲓⲕⲁⲛ ⲥⲟ̄ⳡ ⲗⲁⲧⲟ̄ⲛ ⲙⲓⲛⳝⲁ ⲉⲛⲛⲓ.
Tuug dukkikan sooy latoon minnga enni.
When the wind blows, what can it take from the tiles?

[Said when you have nothing more to lose.]

(215)

ⳤⲟⲩ̄ⲇⲉ̄ⲛ ⲃ̄ⲁⲃ̄ⲟⲩ ⳝⲉⲗⲗⲓ ⲧⲁⲛⳝⲁ ⲙⲉⲥⲕⲓⲙⲟⲩⲛ.
Fuudeen baabu jelli tannga meskimun.
The father of the scarab will not be tired of his job.[16]

[Said about someone who is a good worker, or advice to someone who tells you to slow down.]

(216)

ⲕⲁⳝⳝⲟⲩ̄ⲛ ⲁⲅⲁⲣⲣⲁ ⲙⲁ̄ⲣⲟ̄ⲅ ⳤⲓ̄ⲣⲓ.
Kaj juun agarra maaroog fiiri.
Wherever the donkey goes, it carries dried dung.

[Said to someone who prefers to continue doing a lowly job rather than improving themselves, or to someone who prefers to continue to work even though they don't have to.]

(217)

ⲥⲉⲅⲉⳊ ⲧⲁⲕⲕⲁ ⲟⲩⲣⲣⲓⲕⲕⲁ ⲕⲁⲃ̄ⲓ.
Seged takka urrikka kabi.
Scorpion only bites who tramples it.

[Advice to be very careful before doing something.]

---

16 The story is about a scarab beetle who made a deal with the moon to marry it, so the moon asked it to cleanse the earth from waste before getting married. This is the reason the scarab is persistent in the hard work of getting rid of the waste.

(218)

Ⲃⲁⲛⲛⲓⲇ ⲙⲁⲥ ⲱⲓⲥⲗⲁⲅⲓⲅ ⲟⲩⲫⲫⲓ ⲧⲁⲛⲛⲁⲧⲟ̄ⲛ ⲟ̄ⲥⲓ.
Banynyid mas wisalngig uffi tannatoon oosi.
Good words make the snake come out from its hole.

[Advice about the effectiveness and magic of sweet talk.]

(219)

ⲁⲃⲟⲗϩⲟⲥⲉ̄ⲛ ⲇⲟⲩⲕⲕⲓ ⲥⲟ̄ⲩⲇⲧⲁ ⲧⲟⲗⲗⲓⲙⲟⲩⲛ.
Abolhoseen dukki suudta tollimun.
A fox does not drag an empty bag.

[Said about someone who can always be found where the benefit is.]

(220)

ⲕⲓⲇⲇⲟⲕⲁ ⲇⲟⲩⲙⲙⲓ ⲕⲓⲇⲇⲁⲫⲓ.
Kiddoka dummi kiddafi.
Who catches a drowned person will drown.

[Advice to avoid danger.]

(221)

ⲇⲉⲅⲉⲣ ⲟⲩⲱⲱⲟⲗⲗⲁ ⲇⲟ̄ⲅⲓ ⲛⲁⲇⲇⲁⲫⲓ.
Deger uwwolla doogi naddafi.
Whoever rides on two saddles will fall.

[Said about someone who has a lot of worries and thinks about them all at the same time, or someone who wants to do two jobs at the same time while that is impossible.]

(222)

ⲕⲁⲣⲕⲁⲡⲉ̄ ⲧⲟ̄ⲩⲅⲕⲁ ⲙ̄ⲡⲙⲟⲩⲛ.
Karkaree tuugka miirmun.
A net[17] does not block the wind.

> [Said about a wasteful person who does not know how to save, or to request the appropriate means to achieve their purpose.]

(223)

ⲙⲟⲩⲅ ⲧⲟⲩⲣⲟⲩⲅⲅⲁ ⲇⲟⲩⲅⲓⲅ ⲟⲩⲛⲛⲟ.
Mug turungnga dungig unno.
A bitch in haste gave birth to blind puppies.

> [Advice not to rush.]

(224)

ⲟⲩⲅⲙⲉ̄ⲅ ⲉⲣⲅⲓ ⳅⲁⲡⲁ̄ⲃⲓⲗ ⲇⲟ̄ⲩ.
Ugmeeg ergi haraabil juu.
He who follows owls reaches ruins.

> [Advice that someone who accompanies the wicked, surely will go to perdition.]

(225)

ⲁⲗⲗⲓ ⲧⲁⲛⲛⲟⲅ ⲙⲓⲧⲧⲁⲡⲡⲁ ⲥⲟⲩⲕⲓⲇⲁⲕⲕⲓⲙⲟⲩⲛ.
Alli tannog mittarra sukidakkimun.
Do not trust his rope to go down into the well.

> [Said about someone who cannot be trusted or relied upon in any work, whether because they are weak or known for their betrayal or limited ability.]

---

17 Referring to a net made of palm leaves. after splitting the leaves in two and made from ropes attached in a special way, it is used to carry cattle feed or weeds from one place to another.

(226)

ⲅⲉⲗⲉⲇⲟ̄ⲛⲁ ⲙⲓⲛⲁ? ⲙⲁⲣⲁⲅ ⲧⲁⲛ ⲙⲓⲛⲁ?
Geledoona mina? Marag tan mina?
What is a wagtail? What is its broth?

[Said to depreciate someone else.]

(227)

ⲛⲁⲣ ⲁⲅⲓⲛ ⲧⲟ̄ⳙⲗ ⲍⲁⲱⲁⲇⲁϳⲁ.
Nar agin tuul hawajaya.
The tongue inside the mouth is a great master.

[Advice to be careful when speaking.]

(228)

ⲕⲓⲋⲋⲁⲇ ⲇⲟⲩⲅⲓ̄ⲇⲕⲁⲛ ⲟⲧⲧⲓⲅ ⳗⲁⲣⲙⲟⲩⲛ.
Kiccad dungijkan ottig farmun.
If the deer gets blinded, he cannot figure out the road.

[If a someone is angry, their anger blinds them from doing the right thing.]

(229)

ⲓⲇⲉ̄ⲛ ⲇⲟ̄ⳙⲛ ⲁⲅⲁⲣⲣⲁ ⲟⳙⳙⲁ̄ⲣⲁ.
Edeen juun agarra oshshaara.
A woman is a servant wherever she goes.

[Said to complain when a man's wife is not taking care her parents-in-law.]

(230)

ⲁⲃⲁⲇⲧⲁ ⲅⲓⲛⲇⲉⲉⲅ ⲁⲱⲁⲧⲉ.
Abadta gindeeg aawate.
Make a fence of thorns for an apple of Sodom.[18]

> [Said about those who exaggerate and do more than a matter needs.]

(231)

Oⲩⲗⲟⲩⲙⲙⲁ ⲃⲁⲍⲁⲣⲣⲁ ⲁⲛⲅⲛⲅⲓⲓ ⲓⲓⲅⲓⲛⲛⲁ.
Ulumma baharra angngii iiginna.
Say uncle to a crocodile in the river

> [Advice that obeying the guardians or rulers is obligatory.]

(232)

ⲉⲱⲣⲟⲟⲕⲁⲛ ⲇⲁⲱⲱⲉ ⲱⲟ ⲅⲁⲗⲃⲁ.
Ewrookan jawwe woo gaalba.
Only cry after it (the waterwheel) works, oh Galba![19]

> [Advice to congratulate someone only after the results are in.]

(233)

ⲥⲉⲣⲣⲁ ⲫⲁ ⲱⲉⲅⲣⲉⳝ ⲅⲟⲩⲣⲉⲣⲣⲁ ⲱⲉⲅⲟⲛ.
Seerra weegrey gureerra weegooson.
Instead of leading him to the barren land, he led him to the fertile one.

> [Said about someone who benefited someone else contrary to their intentions.]

---

18 *Calotropis procera* is a species of flowering plant in the family Apocynaceae that is native to North Africa, tropical Africa, Western Asia, South Asia, and Indochina. The green fruits contain a toxic milky sap that is extremely bitter and turns into a gluey coating which is resistant to soap. Common names for the plant include "apple of Sodom."

19 According to the story, a woman named Galba saw men digging a well for a waterwheel, and was crying of joy so soon that the well collapsed and men were forced to dig again, as soon as they finished the second time, the same woman prepared to shreek again, they told her, "Galba, shreek cries of joy after the waterwheel works."

(234)

Ⲓⲅⲕⲁ Ⲧⲟⲩⲗⲗⲓ Ⲧⲁⲛⲛⲟⲅ Ⲓⲣⲃⲉⲛⲁ.
Iigka tulli tannog irbeena.
Fire is known by its smoke.

[Everything has a specific sign.]

(235)

Ⲓⲇⲉⲛ Ⲛⲁⲥⲥⲓⲕⲕⲁ Ⲉⲇⲧⲁⲙ.
Ideen nassikka edtam.
Do not marry a tall woman.

[Advice not to marry a stronger or richer woman unless you are proper for her.]

(236)

Ⲟⲩⲣⲧⲓ Ⲕⲟⲙⲁⲣⲉⲅ Ⲇⲉⲗⲉⲅ Ⲕⲁⲃⲓ.
Urti koomaareeg jeleg kabi.
A sheep without owner is eaten by a wolf.

[Said about things when they are lost due to lack of monitoring or care.]

(237)

Ⲓⲥⲕⲓⲧⲧⲓⲛ Ⲃⲟⲩⲣⲟⲩϣ Ⲇⲁⲃⲁⲗⲁ Ⲫⲓ.
Iskittin burush dabala fi.
The palm leaf rug of the guest is folded.

[Advice to provide hospitality no matter how long it lasts.]

(238)

ⲦⲀΒⲒⲆ ⲔⲞⲰϪⲔⲒⲢⲖⲞⲄ ⲦⲞ̄ⲢⲀ ⲔⲞⲰϪⲔⲒⲢⲖⲞⲄ ⲪⲀⲖⲞ.
Tabid koshkirlog toora koshkirlog falo.
The blacksmith entered with the long needle[20] and came out with it.

> [Said about someone who has not changed, no matter how many years have passed.]

(239)

ⲀⲖⲖⲒ ⲦⲀⲔⲔⲀ ⲘⲒⲖⲖⲒⲔⲀ ⲘⲞ̄ⲢⲒ.
Alli takka millika moori.
The rope tied the one who twisted it.

> [Said about someone who intends to harm others, but harmed themself.]

(240)

ⲜⲞⲨⲔⲞ̄ⲨⲘⲀⲚ ⲘⲈⲢⲈⲚ ⲈⲆⲆⲒ ⲆⲒ̄ⲤⲔⲀ ⲪⲞ̄ⲄⲘⲞⲨⲚ.
Ḥukuuman meren eddi diiska foogmun.
The hand that the government cuts doesn't bleed.

> [Advice that the ruler's orders are the law and there is no use in opposing them.]

(241)

ⲞⲨ̄ⲤⲔⲀ ⲞⲄⲞ̄ⲢⲀ ⲘⲀⲤⲔⲀ ϬⲒⲖⲖ.
Uuska ogoora maska jill.
Forget evil and remember the good.

> [Advice to be tolerant and forgiving.]

---

20 A needle of more than 15 cm used for the sewing of sails.

(242)

ⲓⲕⲕⲁ ⲕⲁⲃⲟⲛ ⲅⲉ̄ⲣ ⲓⲕⲕⲁ ⲟⲩⲙⲟⲩⲛ.
Ikka kabon geer ikka onymun.
Only the one who tastes from your food cries for you.

[Advice that someone's value is in their work and the good they provide to others.]

(243)

ⲉⲇⲇⲓ ⲥⲟ̄ⲩⲇ ⲕⲁⲥⲥⲁ ⲇⲁ̄ⲇⲇⲁⲕⲕⲟⲩⲙⲟⲩⲛ.
Eddi suud kassa daajdakkumun.
An empty hand is not licked.

[Advice to encourage generosity and giving.]

(244)

ⲟⲩⲣⲟⲩⲇⲗⲁⲧⲟ̄ⲛ ⲕⲟⲩⲥⲉⲇⲁ ⲗⲉ̄ ⲁⲃⲁⲇⲗⲁ ⲇⲉⲅⲉ̄?
Urujlatoon kuseda lee abadla degee?
Do you release the cow from the green field, and tie it to the apples of Sodom?[21]

[Said when denouncing a shift from good to evil.]

(245)

ⲱⲓⲣⲇⲁ ⳝⲓ̄ⲛⲧⲁ̄ⲛ ⲇⲁⲕⲕⲉ̄ⲅ ⲇⲁⲕⲕⲓ.
Wirja fiintaan dakkeeg dakki.[22]
He plays hopscotch naked.

[Said about someone who talks a lot and works a little.]

---

21 *Calotropis procera.*
22 *Handakkee* (*dakkee* is only used in this proverb) is a game played within a square of approximately 10 square meters drawn on the ground between two teams, each team consisting of a king and guards. Each player holds one of his feet with one hand and jumps with the other foot. Whoever reaches the competing team's king and pushes him to the ground or outside the square is the winner. The guards of each team defend their king by preventing the opposing team from reaching it.

(246)

ⲇⲟⲩⲙⲟⲩⲇ ⲧⲟⲩⲫⲫⲓⲇⲁⲕⲕⲟ ⲅⲟⲗⲗⲓⲇⲁⲕ ⲕⲟⲩⲙⲟⲩⲛ.
Jumuud tuffidakko gollidak kumun.
Spit coming out of the mouth is not swallowed.

> [Advice that an obscene word said cannot be undone.]

(247)

ⲅⲓⲛⲇⲉ̄ ⲅⲓⲛⲇⲓⲅ ⲅⲁ̄ⲃⲓⲗⲙⲟⲩⲛ.
gindee gindig gaabilmun.
Thorns do not face thorns.

> [Said about peers who are equal in strength.]

(248)

ⲧⲁⲗⲗⲉ̄ ⲧⲁⲗⲗⲓⲅ ⲕⲟⲃ̄ⲃⲓⲗⲟⲅ ⲅⲁ̄ⲃⲓⲗⲙⲟⲩⲛ.
Tallee tallig koccilog gaabilmun.
The needle does not face the needle with its pointed tip.

> [Said when using a different technique when confronting someone of similar strength.]

(249)

ⲧⲟ̄ⲩⲅ ⲙⲁⲗⲗⲉ̄ ⲥⲓⲅⲓⲣⲕⲁ ⲉⲛⲛⲓⲙⲟⲩⲛ.
Tuug mallee sigirka ennimun.
Not all wind sails the boat.

> [Advice that you can't have all your wishes.]

(250)

ⲁⲥⲥⲁⲣⲓⲛ ϩⲉⲗⲗⲓ ⲉⲇⲇⲓⲅ ⲟⲣⲕⲓⲕⲕⲁⲛⲅⲟ̄ⲛ ⲁⲓ̈ⲅⲁ ⲟⲣⲕⲟⲩⲙⲙⲟⲩⲛ.
Assariin jelli eddig orkikkanngoon ayga orkummun.
If the work of your children cools your hand, it doesn't cool your heart.

> [Advice that if you want a thing well done, do it yourself.]

(251)

ⲕⲟⲥⲥⲓⲛ ⲟⲩⲕⲕⲓ ⲓ̄ⲅⲕⲁ ⲁ̄ⲩⲓⲙⲙⲟⲩⲛ.
Kossin ukki iigka aanyimmun.
Palm leaves don't feed a fire.

> [Advice not to rely on something weak.]

(252)

ⲉⲥⲥⲓⲣ ⲇⲉⲣⲉ̄ⲩⲟ̄ⲕⲁⲛ ⲟⲅⲟ̄ⲇⲙⲟⲩⲛ.
Essir dereenyookan ogoodmun.
When the clay bottle has spilled it does not stand.

> [Said as consolation when a loved one is lost, also to warn/encourage girls about their virginity.]

(253)

ⲓⲥⲕⲓⲧⲧⲓ ⲓⲣⲓⲛ ⲙⲟ̄ⲛⲉⲕⲕⲁ ⲫⲉⲛⲧⲓⲛ ⲛⲟ̄ⲩⲣⲣⲁ ⲟⲥⲕⲓⲣ.
Iskitti irin moonekka fentin nuurra oskir.
Host the guest you dislike in the shade of the palm.

> [Advice how to get rid of an unwanted guest.]

(254)

ⲧⲟⲣⲃⲁⲣ ⲧⲁⲛⲛⲉ̄ⲛⲅⲁ ⲟⲩⲙⲟⲩⲛ.
Torbar tanneenga onymun.
A farmer does not cry about his dead mother.

> [Said about someone who is always busy.]

(255)

ⲧⲟⲣⲃⲁⲣⲕⲁ ⲉⲇⲇⲓⲅ ⲟⲩⲥⲟⲩⲣⲣⲁ ⲟⲩⲇⲓⲣⲧⲉ̄ⲛⲁⲅ̄ⲟ̄ⲛ ⲛⲉⲱⲗⲁⲓ̈ⲁ.
Torbarka eddig usurra udirteenangoon neshlaya.
Help the farmer, even by putting your hand in his ass.

> [Advice to accept any help, no matter how trivial or strange.]

(256)

ⲅⲟⲩⲥⲥⲉ̄ⲅ̄ⲟ̄ⲛ ⲇⲁⲃⲁⲗⲕⲁⲛ ⲓⲣⲕⲓ ⲧⲁⲛⲛⲁⲧⲟ̄ⲛ ⲫⲁ.
Gusseegoon dabalkan irki tannatoon fa.
The silo, if rolled, can be removed from its place.

> [Advice that there is no difficulty in doing anything if there is a will and a subtle trick.]

(257)

ⲟ̄ⲩⲥⲓⲛ ⲅⲁⲥⲕⲟⲧⲟ̄ⲛ ⲙⲁⲥⲧⲟ̄ⲇⲧⲁ ⲃⲁ̄ⲓ̈ⲉ̄ⲛⲛⲁ.
Uusin gaskotoon mastoodta baayeenna.
Amid evil the good appears.

> [Advice that the difference between good and bad is as clear as the sun.]

(258)

ⲧⲟⲩⲅⲕⲁ ⲧⲁⲣⲓⲛ ⲕⲓⲣⲉⲗⲟⲅ ⲥⲓⲗⲗⲁ ⲧⲓⲣ.
Tuugka tarin kirelog silla tir.
Scattering the crops in the direction of the wind.

[Said about the need to adapt and socialize.]

(259)

ⲫⲟⲅⲣⲓⲛ ⲧⲓ̄ ⲃⲁⲅⲁ̄ⲛⲓⲗ ⲟ̄ⲓ̄ⲅⲁ ⲟⲩⲇⲉ.
Fogrin tii bagaanyil ooyga ude.
The unfortunate cow steps into a crack.

[Said about those who have had misfortune or bad luck.]

(260)

ⲧⲟ̄ⲩⲛ ⲅⲟⲩⲣⲣⲓⲕⲁⲛ ϫⲟⲣⲉ̄ ⲁⲃⲇⲉ̄.
Tuun gurrikan joree abdee.
If the inside is happy, the hair grows.

[Advice to imitate the happiness of your neighbors and community.]

ⲧⲟ̄ⲩⲛ ⲅⲟⲩⲣⲣⲓⲕⲁⲛ ⲅⲟⲩⲣⲣⲉ̄ ⲁⲃⲁⲇⲉ̄.
Tuun gurrikan gurree abadee.
If the inside is happy, be happy and dance.

[Advice to imitate the happiness of your neighbors and community.]

(261)

ⲉ̄ⲛⲅⲁ ⲕⲟⲩⲛⲓ ⲱⲓⲣϫⲁ/ⲟⲣⲅⲁ ⲫⲓ̄ⲟⲩⲙⲟⲩⲛ.
Eenga kuni wirja/orga fiyumun.
Who has their mother does not sleep uncovered/hungry.

[Used to recall the care of a mother when her absence is felt.]

(262)

Ⲃⲁⲯⲯⲓⲥⲟⲩⲛ ⲙⲁⲗⲗⲉ̄ⲕⲕⲁ ⲅⲟⲣ ẟⲟⲕⲕⲉⲃ̄ⲃ̄ⲟ.
Banynyisun malleekka gor jokkecco.
The calf chewed everything we said.

       [Said about a lost effort, gone with the wind.]

(263)

Ⲫⲉⲛⲧⲓⲗⲗⲁⲧⲟ̄ⲛ ⲥⲟⲩⲕⲕⲁ ⲁⲕⲕⲟⲯⲓⲗ Ⲇⲁⲣⲣⲓ.
Fentillatoon sukka akkonyil darri.
He came down from the palm tree and climbed the castor tree.

       [Said about someone who blabbers and mixes up words.]

(264)

Ⲓⲥⲥⲉ̄ ⳅⲁⲙⲓ̄ⲣⲁⲇⲇⲁⲛ ⲕⲟⲩⳗⳗⲓ.
Issee hamiiraddan kushshi.
The dough rises after adding the yeast.

       [Said when seeking something for the right reasons.]

(265)

Ⲟⲯⲓⲛ ⲛⲟ̄ⲅⲓⲗ Ⲃⲁⲗⲉ̄ ⲁ̄ⲱⲇⲁⲕⲕⲟⲩⲙⲟⲩⲛ.
Onyin noogil balee aawdakkumun.
In the house of mourning, a wedding cannot be held.

       [Advice that one's actions have to be appropriate to the general mood.]

(266)

ⲕⲁⲙⲙ ⲁⲅ ⲛⲁ̄ⲛⲧⲁ̄ⲛ ⲟ̄ⲓ̈ ⲧⲁⲛⲅⲁ ⲧⲓⲅⲓ.
Kamm aag naantaan ooy tannga tigi.
He is tracking the camel though he sees it.

> [Said about someone who strains themself in a useless act, or who chooses the bumpy over the paved road to reach a goal.]

(267)

ⲁⲅⲟⲛⲇⲉ̄ⲛ ⲟⲃⲟⲣ ⲥⲓⲃⲉ̄ⲅ ⲓⲥⲕⲓⲣⲙⲟⲩⲛ.
Agondeen obor sibeeg iskirmun.
The root of the lupine does not gather the clay.

> [Said about someone whom you should not have high expectations of.]

(268)

ⲅⲟⲩⲧⲣⲁ̄ⲛ ⲇⲁ̄ⲇⲓ̄ ⲟⲩⲅⲓⲣⲁⲅⲙⲟⲩⲛ.
Gutraan daadii ungirangmun.
The smell of the tar container will not go away.
Habit ever remains.

> [Advice that any trait someone develops is difficult to get rid of.]

(269)

ⲧⲉⲙⲉ̄ⲛ ⲕⲉⲫⲫⲓ ⲱⲓⲥⲕⲓⲇⲁ.
Temeen keffi wiskida.
The slap of the neighbor is returned.

> [Advice that abuse of a neighbor is intolerable.]

Proverbs

89

(270)

ⲦⲈⲘⲈ̄Ⲛ ⲔⲈⳞⳞⲒ ⲞⲢⲔⲘⲞⲨⲚ.
Temeen keffi orkmun.
The slap of the neighbor will not cool.

[Advice that abuse of a neighbor is intolerable.]

(271)

ⳞⲞ̄ⲅⲆⲞ ⲘⲒⲖⲖⲒⲘⲞⲨⲚ.
Foogjo middimun.
What is spilled will not return to the pot.

[Missed can not be returned.]

(272)

ⲒⲚⲈ̄Ⲛ ⲦⲞ̄Ⲗ ⲒⲔⲔⲀ ⲒⲚⲈ̄Ⲛ ⲦⲞ̄ⲖⲦⲀ ⲞⲨⲚⲚⲀ ⲦⲒⲢⲘⲞⲨⲚ.
Ineen tood ikka ineen toodta unna tirmun.
Your mother's son[23] can't give you a mother's son.

[Advice that siblings cannot be replaced.]

(273)

ⲦⲞ̄ⲨⲄ ⲖⲞⲨⲔⲔⲒⲔⲀⲚ ⲘⲒⲦⲦⲀⲢⲒⲚ ⲦⲞ̄ⲨⲖⲄⲞ̄Ⲛ ⲖⲞⲨⲔⲔⲒ.
Tuug dukkikan mittarin tuulgoon dukki.
If the wind blows, it blows even in the well.

[Advice about the spreading of news and its ability to overcome barriers.]

---

23   I.e., brother.

(274)

Ⲫⲁ ⲕⲟⲩⲋⲋⲓⲛⲧⲁ̄ⲛ ⲓ̄ⲅⲕⲁ ⲁ̄ⲅ ⲕⲁⲕⲕⲓ.
Fa kuccintaan iigka aag kakki.
He will swim and sit next to the fire.

> [Said about someone who cannot evaluate what is he going to do next.]

(275)

ⲟⲧⲧⲓⲛ ⲁⲅⲟ ⲅⲟ̄ⲩⲣⲁⲛ ⲇⲓ̄ⲛⲁ̄ⲣⲁ.
Ottin ago guuran diinaara.
A daughter's husband is an ornament on her mother-in-law's forehead.

> [Advice about the value of a son-in-law.]

(276)

ⲉⲇⲇⲓ ⲙⲁⲅⲁ̄ⲇ ⲱⲉ̄ⲕⲁ ⲉⲛⲛⲓ.
Eddi magaad weeka enni.
A hand holds one watermelon.

> [Said about someone who tries to work or endure more than they can.]

(277)

ⲁⲣⲓϫ ⲇⲉⲥⲥⲓⲕⲕⲁ ⲓⲇ ⲓⲛⲅⲁ ⲁⲙⲁⲛⲧⲓⲧⲧⲁⲙ.
Arij dessikka id innga amantittam.
Don't show your husband raw meat.

> [Advice to a wife to avoid giving a reason to her husband to become angry.]

(278)

ⴰⵎⴰⵏ ⴰⵢⴽⴽⵉ ⵜⴰⵏⵏⵓⴳ ⵡⴻⴽⴰ ⴽⵓⴼⴼⵉⵎⵓⵢⵏ.
Aman ukki tannog weeka koffimun.
He is not worth the water that fills his ears.

[Said about a worthless person.]

(279)

ⴽⴰⵢⵢⴻⴳ ⴰⴳ ⴽⴰⵔⵉⵏ ⵉⴳ ⴷⵉⴷⵓⵏ.
Kashsheeg aag kaarin iig diijon.
The fire went out while they were collecting firewood.

[Said when someone clumsily fails to achieve what is required of them.]

(280)

ⵛⴰⴷⵓⵏ ⵉⵛⴽⴻⵏⵜⴻ ⴰⵡⵡⵓⵏ ⵉⵛⴽⴻⵏⵜⴻⴳ ⵜⵓⵢⵒⵉ.
Shaadon iskentee awwon iskenteeg turi.
The foreign mouse throws out the house mouse.

[Said when a stranger drives you out of your house.]

(281)

ⵛⴰⴷⵓⵏ ⵉⵛⴽⴻⵏⵜⴻ ⴰⵡⵡⵓⵏ ⵉⵛⴽⴻⵏⵜⴻⴳ ⵜⵉⵛⵛⵉ.
Shaadon iskentee awwon isskenteeg tissi.
The mouse from the outside hates the mouse from the inside.

[Said about a newcomer trying to ingratiate themself at the expense of others.]

(282)

ⲧⲟⲩⲅ ⲙⲁⲗⲗⲉ̄ ⲟⲩⲣ ⲧⲁⲛⲅⲁ ⲅⲟⲩⲯⲯⲓⲕⲓⲣⲙⲟⲩⲛ.
Tuug mallee ur tanga gonynyikirmun.
No wind can shake his head.

[Said about a stubborn, strong-minded man you can count on.]

(283)

ⲁⲥⲉⲇⲓ ⲗⲁⲧⲟ̄ⲛ ⲕⲟⲩϣⲁⲣ ϥⲁⲙⲙⲟⲩ.
Asedi latoon kushar fammu.
The stem of a wheat plant does not make keys.[24]

[Advice to choose the right thing.]

(284)

ⲃⲁⲍⲁⲣ ⲕⲟ̄ⲛ ⲧⲓⲃⲓⲇ ⲕⲓⲯⲯⲓⲛ ϥⲁ ⲕⲟⲩϣⲩϳⲓⲇⲟⲛ.
Bahar koon tibid kinynyin fakoshshijon.
The river will rot without waves.

[Advice to always keep yourself occupied.]

(285)

ⲉⲥⲕⲁⲗⲉ̄ ϥⲉ̄ϣⲉ̄ ⲱⲉ̄ⲗⲟⲅ ⲙⲓⲛϫⲓⲙⲟⲩⲛ.
eskalee feeshee weelog minjimun.
The water wheel does not stop for one hopper.[25]

[Advice that group work is not disrupted by one of its members.]

---

24 The doors of the houses in old Nubia were huge and had wooden locks, in the shape of the letter L, with slightly obtuse angle wooden keys.
25 All water wheel have a number of hoppers, these hoppers number varies depending on the nature and depth of the well, and the number of hoppers in the sommelier may reach forty saints.If some break down, the water wheel will working.

(286)

ⲕⲓⲧⲧⲓⲛ ẟⲉⲛẟⲓ ⲉλλⲁⲅⲙⲟⲩⲛ.
Kittin jenbi eddangmun.
Not all clothing parts work as a sleeve.

> [Advice that each part fits its own.]

(287)

ⲍⲁⲣⲓⲣ ⲫⲁⲣ ⲕⲁẟⲓⲛ ⲱⲉλⲁⲅⲓ.
Hariir faar kajin weedangi.
Old silk becomes the saddle of the donkey.

> [Said about someone whose fame has faded.]

(288)

ⲕⲟⲅⲓⲛ ⲱⲟλλⲁ ⲅⲟⲛ ⲫⲁϊⲁ ⲫⲓⲙⲟⲩⲛ.
Koogin shoolla goon faaya fiimun.
This is not written even in the crow's message.[26]

> [Said about unusual supernatural matters.]

(289)

ẟⲟⲩλλⲉ̄ ⲫⲁⲕⲕⲁⲛ ⲅⲓⲛλⲉ̄ ⲧⲁⲛλⲁⲛ ⲫⲁ.
Jullee fakkan gindee tandan fa.
An acacia tree grows with its thorns.

> [Advice that something has both a good and a bad side, take it or leave it.]

---

26 As the story is told, some women were angry that men have the right to polygamy, but women not, so they went to the crow and told their story, asking him to return their rights. The crow said: "This is easy. Write a message with this, and I will take it to the Lord and I will return soon." They wrote the message. The crow flew to the heavens, but did not return, while the women are still waiting.

(290)

ⲕⲟⲩ ⲕⲟⲯⲯⲁ ⲫⲉ̄ⲓ̈.
Kony konynya feey.
Face meets face.

[Advice that direct contact and clarity is the best way to solve problems.]

(291)

ⲫⲟ̄ⲩⲇⲉ̄ ⲟⲩⲣ ⲃⲁϭϭⲁⲫⲓ̄ⲛ ⲧⲁⲯⲯⲓ.
Fuudee ur baccafiin tanynyi.
The ladybug walks even if its head is crushed.

[Said about those who continuously survive harm.]

(292)

ⲁⲥⲥⲁⲣ ⲧⲟ̄ⲩ ⲕⲁⲱⲱⲁⲫⲓ̄ⲛ ⲧⲁⲯⲯⲓ.
Assar tuu kawwafiin tanynyi.
The child walks with his belly open.

[Said when someone is ignorant of the seriousness of a situation or its consequences.]

(293)

ⲁⲙⲁⲛ ⲫⲁ̄ⲗⲁ ⲱⲉ̄ⲗⲁ ⲕⲓⲇⲇⲓ.
Aman faala weela kiddi.
To sink into a bowl of water.

[Said when shows failure or weakness in the face of a problematic situation.]

(294)

꜡oyʌʌē мāмē ᴛᴀɴɴoг Ɔejji.
Jullee maamee tannog feyyi.
The tree grows with its roots.

> [Advice to rely on oneself.]

(295)

꜡eʌʌiг ꜡āгi ᴋᴀƁᴀᴋᴋᴀ ᴋᴀƁмoyɴ.
Jellig jaagi kabakka kabmun.
He who is afraid of work will not eat.

> [Advice that encourages and glorifies work.]

(296)

ᴀɴēɴ Ⲇijeʌeᴋiɴ ᴀɴēɴ Ɓeciɴ Ⲇije гeɴᴀ.
Aneen diyelekin aneen besin diye gena.
Better that my aunt die than my mother.

> [Advice to choose the lesser evil.]

(297)

iɴēɴ ᴛōⲆ iᴋᴋᴀ мōɴмoyɴ.
Ineen tood ikka moonmun.
Your mother's son[27] does not hate you.

> [Advice about the strength of the kinship bond between brothers.]

---

27 I.e., brother.

(298)

Ⲓⲅ ⲕⲟⲩⲆⲟ̄ⲩⲆⲦⲀ ⲕⲟⲙⲙⲟⲩⲚ.
Iig kuduudta kommun.
A small fire does not exist.

[Advice not to underestimate the little things.]

(299)

Ⲃⲟⲩⲣⲟ̄ⲩ ⲅⲟ̄ⲛ ⲕⲟⲩⲆⲟ̄ⲩⲆⲦⲀ ⲕⲟⲩⲙⲙⲟⲩⲚ.
Buruu goon kuduudta kummun.
A girl isn't young.

[Advice to protect girls as if they are an adult even if they're young.]

(300)

ⲈⲖⲒⲚ ⲅⲟⲣ ⲦⲞ̄Ⲇ ⲰⲀⲖⲖⲞⲚ ⲦⲒ̄ ⲦⲞ̄Ⲇ.
Elin gor tood wallon tii tood.
Today's calf is tomorrow's cow.

[Advice that what you underestimate today, you will seek tomorrow.]

(301)

ⲘⲞⲅⲞⲣ ⲕⲟⲩⲆⲈ̄ ⲦⲀⲚⲚⲀ ⲦⲞ̄Ⲛ Ⲃⲟⲗⲟⲗⲓ
Mogor kudee tanna toon bololi.
A billygoat out of his corral makes a *bololi* sound.[28]

[Upbringing and ethics, home is the first place to teach ethics.]

---

28 The sound a billygoat makes when he's horny.

(302)

κᾱιуcαΝΔο κογιуιуα κογΜΜογΝ.
Kaashsando kushsha kummun.
Since it was kneaded, it didn't rise.

> [Said about someone who despite investment of time and energy does not perform.]

(303)

δo͞гo ᾱгιΝ ΝιФФο ΛᾱδO.
Joogo aagin niffo daajo.
The miller tasted it before the cook.

> [Said when someone is deprived of their right, because its given to someone who does not deserve it.]

(304)

ϐοгΔο κᾱjēΛ κΑϐι.
Bogdo kaayeel kabi.
The pottery maker eats in a broken bowl.

> [Said about someone who fixes others people's things but forgets their own.]

(305)

ιcκιττι ФΑcιΛ ΤΑΝΝοг κι.
Iskitti fasil tannog ki.
The guest comes with food.

> [Advice to encourage hospitality.]

(306)

ⲧⲁⲧⲧⲟⲩⲣⲓⲛ ⲇⲟⲩ ⲫⲁⲥⲥⲓⲅⲓⲙⲟⲩⲛ.
Tattuurin juu fassingimun.
A bitter apple will not be sweet.

[Advice that someone who grew up evil remains like this.]

(307)

ⲓⲅ ⲟⲩⲃⲟⲩⲣⲧⲓⲅ ⲟⲩⲛⲛⲓ.
Iig uburtig unni.
Fire bears ash.

[Said when the outcome of a situation was easy to predict.]

(308)

ⲕⲉⲣⲣⲓ ⲟⲩ̄ ⲱⲉ̄ⲗⲟⲅ ⲙⲉⲛⲇⲓⲙⲟⲩⲛ.
Kerri ooy weelog menjimun.
A tent does not stand on a single pole.

[Advice that work needs synergy.]

(309)

ⲇⲟⲩⲅⲅⲓ ⲇⲟⲩⲅⲅⲓⲅ ⲟⲩⲛⲓⲙⲟⲩⲛ.
Dungngi dungngig unnimun.
A blind person does not give birth to the blind.

[Advice that children do not necessarily take after their parents.]

(310)

ⲅⲟⲣⲟⲛⲇⲓ ⲫⲓ̄ⲛⲧⲁ̄ⲛ ⲓⲣⲣⲓ.
Gorondi fiintaan irri.
The bull bellows while he is lying.

[Said about someone who threatens without doing anything.]

(311)

ⲁⲱⲣⲓ̄ⲛ ⲕⲟⲯⲩⲁ ϫⲉⲗⲱⲁ ⲗⲉ̄ ⲛⲓ̄ⲛⲁ.
Ashriin konynya jelwa lee niina.
Do we drink and wash the face of the beautiful woman?

> [Advice not to depend on your beauty alone.]

(312)

ⲁⲣⲁⲅⲓ ⲕⲟⲯⲩⲁ ⲧⲓⲅⲓⲣⲙⲟⲩⲛ.
Aragi konynya tigirmun.
Who dances does not hide their face.

> [Said about those who are not ashamed of their behavior.]

(313)

ⲟⲩⲇⲣⲟ̄ⲥⲁⲙ ⲕⲁⲃⲓⲛⲛⲁ.
Udroosam kabinna.
Bake before you eat.

> [Advice that you have to put in the work if you want results.]

(314)

ⲛⲁⲣ ⲧⲟ̄ⲩⲛ ⲅⲉⲗⲉⲙⲁ.
Nar tuun gelema.
The tongue is the belly's pen.

> [Advice that your tongue expresses your thoughts.]

(315)

ⲫⲁⲅ ϫⲟ̄ⲩⲣⲧⲉ̄ⲅ ⲕⲁⲃⲁⲫⲓ̄ ⲛⲁⲱⲁ ⲧⲁⲛⲛⲁ ⲃⲓ̄ⲛⲛⲁ.
Fag juurteeg kabafii nawa tanna biinna.
A goat that eat acacia tree fruits shows it by her skin.

> [Advice that what you hide today will definitely appear tomorrow.]

(316)

ⲚⲁⲂⲓⲔⲔⲞⲚ ⲚⲓⲘ ⲔⲓⲤⲤⲈⲀ ⲪⲒ.
Nabikkoon nim kisseel fii.
Even gold you find in the ruins of a church.[29]

[Advice not to expect a good result without doing your job.]

(317)

ⲀⲂⲖⲓⲤⲈⲚ ⲈⲢⲢⲈ ⲦⲀⲚⲄⲀ ⲆⲈⲰⲀ ⲒⲄⲤⲀⲚⲆⲞ ⲘⲞⲨⲖⲈⲚ ⲔⲞⲂⲂⲒⲖ ⲆⲞⲨ ⲆⲞⲢⲢⲞ.
Abliseen erree tannga dewaa iigsando muuleen koccil juu jorro.
When fox was told that his urine is a cure, he climbed up the mountain and urinated over it.

[Said about someone who is stingy with what they have and does not want others to benefit from it.]

(318)

ⲔⲀⲘⲒⲔⲔⲀ ⲆⲈⲄⲈⲢⲒⲚ ⲦⲀⲰⲰⲞ ⲀⲄⲔⲀⲢⲒ.
Kamikka degerin tawwoo aagkaari.
Looking for the camel under the saddle.

[Said about someone who looking for something while it is right under his nose.]

(319)

ⲔⲀⲢⳜⲒⲢⲀⲖⲖⲈⳖ ⲆⲞⲨⲄⲀⲂⲂⲞ.
Karjiralley jugacco.
She wanted to cook food and burned it.

[Said about someone clumsy trying to fix something but instead destroying it.]

---

[29] This refers to the many medieval church ruins in Nubia and the widespread belief that they contained treasures.

(320)

ⲃoyⲣoy ⲦⲀⲚⲚⲈ̄Ⲛ Ⲛō̄ⲅⲓⲗ ⲓⲥⲕⲓⲦⲦⲁ.
Buru tanneen noogil iskitta.
The girl is a guest at her mother's house.

> [Advice that it's only a matter of time until a girl gets married.]

(321)

ⲕⲁⲇ̄̄ⲓⲥ ⲙoⲡⲓ̄ ⲇⲉⲇⲓⲗ Ⲧō̄ⲡⲙoyⲚ.
kadiis morii jeebil toormun.
A wild cat does not enter your pocket.

> [Advice not to trust a stranger.]

(322)

ⲥō̄yⲗⲦō̄Ⲛ ⲓⲦⲦⲓⲡⲗⲁ Ⲧⲁⲫⲫⲓ.
Suultoon ittirla taffi.
To taste from the milk to the *ittir*.[30]

> [Said when someone suddenly switches the topic of a conversation without finishing.]

(323)

ⲁⲗⲗⲓ ⲫⲁ̄ⲥⲉ̄ ⲙⲓⲗⲗⲓⲕⲁⲚ ⲕoyⲦⲦⲁ ⲙⲓⲚⲇⲓⲙoyⲚ.
Alli faasee millikan kutta minjimun.
The weak twisted rope does not stand upright.

> [Said about someone with a weak personality.]

---

30 See fn. 13.

(324)

ⲫⲉⲕⲕⲉ̄ⲛ ⲁⲗⲗⲓ ⲙⲓⲗⲗⲓⲕⲁⲛ ⲕⲟⲩⲧⲧⲓⲙⲟⲩⲛ.
fekkeen alli millikan kuttimun.
A twisted rope of old cloth does not stand upright.

[Said about someone with a weak personality.]

(325)

ⲙⲁⲣⲉ̄ ⳣⲁ̄ⲣⲟ̄ⲛⲕⲁⲛ ⲛⲟ̄ⲩⲇⲧⲁ ⲟ̄ⲥⲓⲛ.
Maree shaaroonkan nuudta oosin.
If you reduce the number of corn plants in the basin, they produce the best fruits.

[Advice that a few being productive are better than many but less productive.]

(326)

ϫⲟⲩⲙⲁ ⲙⲁⲥ ⵣⲁⲙⲓ̄ⲥⲗⲁⲧⲟ̄ⲛ ⲃ̌ⲓⲛⲓ.
Juma mas hamiislatoon biini.
A good Friday is known from Thursday.

[Advice that the ending of things shows earlier on.]

(327)

ⲧⲁ̄ⲧⲉ̄ⲇ ⲟⲥⲥⲟ̄ⲩ ⲕⲓⳣⳣⲓⲛ ⲙⲉⲛϫⲓⲙⲟⲩⲛ.
Taateeb ossuu kinynyin menjimun.
Wooden beams on the ceiling must have a pillar.

[Advice that everything has a basis to rely on.]

(328)

ᴀppi cī͞ʙᴀϕīκᴀ ðᴀ͞г.
Arri siibafiika jaag.
Beware of still water.

> [Advice to be cautious with calm or silent people,
> since they may be deceptive and cunning.]

(329)

ᴀмᴀɴ ɴē͞pᴀϕīκᴀ ðᴀ͞г.
Aman neerafiika jaag.
Beware of stagnant water.

> [Advice to be cautious with calm or silent people,
> since they may be deceptive and cunning.]

(330)

κᴀм κᴀʙᴀʌог κejĩмоyɴ.
Kam kabalog keyimun.
The camel did not grow up by eating.

> [Advice that things might happen without
> logical or reliable reason.]

(331)

гiɴλiг гiɴλēɴ г͞ēp λoyκκiмоyɴ.
Gindig gindin geer dukkimun.
Thorns can only be removed by thorns.

> [Advice to fight fire with fire.]

(332)

ⲦⲈⲘⲈ̄Ⲛ ⲆⲒⲦⲦⲒ ⲆⲉⲅⲆⲁⲕⲕⲓⲙⲟⲩⲛ.
Temeen jitti degdakkimun.
The *jitti*[31] of a neighbor cannot be worn.

> [Advice not to show off something that you don't own, or to pretend to be someone you're not.]

(333)

ⲘⲁⲕⲕⲁⲆⲁⲛ ⲁⲅⲁⲣⲣⲁ ⲛⲟⲅⲟ.
Makkadan agarra nogo.
It became empty like a maize field after harvest.

> [Said when crowded place suddenly became empty.]

(334)

ⲁⲃⲁ̄ⲅⲟⲩⲛⲛⲁ ⲁⲃⲁⲆⲓⲗⲟⲛ ⲫⲟⲗⲗⲓⲙⲉ̄ⲛⲁ.
Abaagunna abadilon foddimeena.
If I die, even the apple of Sodom[32] will not grow.

> [Curse that nothing may grow or flourish after someone's departure.]

(335)

ⲃⲁ̄Ⲇⲟⲩⲛⲛⲁ ⳉⲁⲙⲃⲁⲣⲦⲉ̄ⲗⲟ̄ⲛ ⲫⲟⲗⲗⲓⲙⲉ̄ⲛⲁ.
Baadunna hambarteeloon foddimeena.
If I die, even saw sedge[33] will not grow.

> [Curse that nothing may grow or flourish after someone's departure.]

---

31 A *jitti* is a specific type of golden necklace.
32 *Calotropis procera.*
33 *Cladium mariscus.*

(336)

ⲕⲁⲱⲱⲉ̄ ⲇⲓⲅⲓⲛⲧⲉ̄ⲅ ⲇⲟ̄ⲗⲧⲁⲙ.
Kashshee diginteeg dooltam.
Do not harvest different types of vegetables at the same time.

> [Advice not to jump from tree to tree.]

(337)

ⲟ̄ⲉ́ⲓⲗ ⲫⲁ̄ⲓ́ⲁⲫⲓ̄ⲕⲁ ⲕⲟⲯⲓⲗ ⲫⲁ̄ⲓ́ⲧⲁⲙ.
Ooyil faayafiika konyil faaytam.
Do not write on your face what is written on your feet.

> [Advice that not participating in events may make you face blame.]

(338)

ⲛⲟ̄ⲣ ⲕⲓⲃ̄ⲃⲁⲇⲧⲁ ⳅⲓⲗⲅⲟ̄ⲥⲁ ⲙⲟⲣⲉ ⲱⲉ̄ⲕⲁ ⳅⲓⲗⲅⲁⲧⲉ̄.
Noor kiccadta hilgoosa more weeka hilgatee.
God created deer and a tree (to feed it).

> [Advice about the providence of God and his great mercy for his creatures.]

(339)

ⲙⲟ̄ⲩⲣ ϫⲁⲱⲁⲣⲁⲓ́ ⲓⲇ ⲓⲛⳝⲁ ⲫⲁⲯⲓⲛ ⲟⲩⲥⲕⲓⲣⲧⲁⲙ.
Muur jawaray id inga fanyin uskirtam.
Do not argue that the firewood is soft and does not burn, leaving your husband without a dinner.

> [Advice to avoid upsetting one's husband.]

(340)

ⲥⲉⲅⲉⲇⲓⲛ ⲟⲩⲫⲫⲓⲗ ⲉⲇⲇⲓⲅ ⲟⲩⲇⲓⲣⲧⲁⲙ.
Segedin uffil eddig udirtam.
Do not put your hand in the hole of scorpion.

[Advice to avoid dangers.]

(341)

ⲟⲩⲧⲧⲟⲩ̄ⲛⲓⲗⲟⲅ ⲓⲛⲛⲓⲅ ⲓⲣⲱ.
Uttuunilog innig irny.
Keep your belongings among others' belongings.

[Advice to benefit from others' opinions and experiences.]

(342)

ⲛⲁⲣ ⲧⲁⲅⲅⲁ ⲙⲟⲩⲣⲧⲙⲟ̄ⲩⲛⲓ ⲁⲓ̈ ⲧⲁⲅⲅⲁ ⲙⲟⲩⲣⲧⲟⲩⲙⲟⲩⲛ.
Nar tangnga murtumuuni ay tangnga murtumon.
He who does not control his tongue does not control his heart.

[Advice to know when to speak and when to shut up.]

(343)

ⲃⲁⲱⲓⲇ ⲕⲁⲇϭⲁ ⲫⲉⲛⲧⲓⲁ ⲕⲉ̄ⲣⲕⲉⲕⲕⲁ ⲃⲁⲱⲓ.
Banynyid kajca fentil keerkekka banynyi.
His words make the donkey climb up the palm tree.

[Said about someone talking nonsense.]

(344)

ⲓⲕⲕⲁ ⲇⲓⲅϭⲁⲧⲉ̄ ⲗⲉⲕⲓⲛ ⲓⲕⲕⲁ ⲟⲱⲕⲉ̄ ⲇⲟⲗⲗⲓⲛⲁ.
Ikka jigjatee lekin ikka onykee dollina.
The one who makes you cry love you more than the one who makes you laugh.

[Advice to appreciate those who are honest in their criticism.]

(345)

ⲟⲩⲃⲟⲩⲣⲧⲓⲛ ⲫⲓⲛ ⲁⲅⲁⲣⲣⲁ ⲛⲓⲗⲗⲓ ⲱⲁ̄ⲥⲁ ⲧⲟ̄ⲣⲓ.
Uburtin fiin agarra nilli waasa toori.
In the place of ash, a lot of coals enter.

> [Said when a group of drunks is joined by another drunk, or when bad news is added to already bad news.]

(346)

Ⲇⲟⲩⲅⲅⲓⲛ ⲙⲁ̄ⲣⲣⲁ ⲅⲟⲩϣⲕⲟⲩ ⲅⲁ̄ⲗⲓ̇ⲁ.
dungngin maarra goshku gaaliya
In the alley of the blind the one-eyed is precious.

> [Advice that those who are skilled are valuable among those who are not.]

(347)

Ⲓⲇⲉ̄ⲛ Ⲇⲟ̄ⲩϣ ⳓⲁⲧⲁⲃⲁⲛ ⲕⲓⲇⲓⲗ ⲙⲁ̄ⲣⲣⲁ ⲕⲟⲗⲟⲇⲧⲁ ⲟⲩϣⲉ̄ⲛ.
Ideen doosh hataban kidil marra kolodta usheen.
A stupid woman hits the doorpost seven times.

> [Used when someone repeats the same mistake over and over.]

(348)

ⲟⲩⲃⲟⲩⲣⲧⲓ ⲧⲁⲕⲕⲁ ⲛⲟ̄ⲓ̇ⲟⲕⲕⲁ ⲕⲟⲗⲗⲓ.
Uburti takka nooyokka kolli.
Ash gets stuck with the one who spoils it.

> [Advice that who does evil to harm others and harm themself.]

(349)

ⲕⲓⲇⲇⲁ ⲇⲟⲣⲟ ⲧⲓⲃⲓⲇⲧⲁ ⲇⲁⲅⲙⲟⲩⲛ.
Kidda jooro tibidta jaagmun.
A drowning man is not afraid of the waves.

[Said about someone who faces big problems and is not bothered by the small ones.]

(350)

ⲛⲁⲣ ⲁⲛⲛⲁ ϣⲉⲅⲉⲣⲧⲓ ⲫⲉϳⲟⲛⲁ.
Nar anna shengerti feyona.
Hair grew on my tongue.

[Said after a lot of talking.]

(351)

ⲥⲉⲣⲓⲓⲅⲁ ⲕⲁⲃⲁⲫⲓⲛ ⲧⲟⲩ ⲟⲣⲟⲙⲁⲫⲓ.
Seriinga kapafiin tuu oromafi.
The stomach of who eats barley felt cold.

[Said when someone who has done something wrong overhears other people talking about in general and feels as if it pertains to themself.]

(352)

ⲛⲁⲃⲗⲁⲧⲟⲛ ϩⲓⲇⲓⲗⲕⲁ ⲕⲁϳⲕⲁⲅⲟⲛ ⲟϣϣⲁ ⲧⲟⲩⲣⲕⲟⲩⲙⲁⲅⲙⲟⲩⲛ.
Naablatoon hijilka kaykangoon oshsha turkumaangmun.
Even if the servant dresses in an anklet of gold, she will not become an Ottoman lady.[34]

[Advice that newly acquired wealth does not necessarily come with good manners.]

---

[34] The Ottoman Empire ruled Egypt from 1517 to 1867, apart from the period of the French occupation from 1798 to 1801.

(353)

ⵉⵏⴳⴰⵏ ⵏⴰ ⵉⴳⴰⵜⴰⵏⴰ.
Inngoon nee iingateena?
Do you listen to this (useless stuff) as well?

> [Said when someone is talking about superfluous things.]

(354)

ⵉⵏⴳⴰ ⴼⴰⴽⵉⵏ ⴰⵎⴱⵉⴳⴰⵍ ⵜⴰⴼⴼⵉ ⵡⴰⵍⵍⴰ ⴰⴳⵉⵍ ⴼⵓⴷⴻ?
Ingnga fakin ambigal taffi walla agil fudee?
Are you going to throw this at the dom palm tree or you will you put it in your mouth?[35]

> [Advice not to take big bites while eating.]

(355)

ⵎⵓⵔⵜⵉ ⴰⵙⵙⴰⵔⵜⴰⵏⴳⴰ ⵊⴰⴽⴽⵓⵎⵓⵏ.
Murti assartanga jakkumun.
A horse does not trample on his newborn.

> [Said about the compassion and mercy of motherhood.

(356)

ⴽⴻⴽⴽⵓⵓ ⴳⵓⵏ ⴽⴻⴽⴽⴰ ⴷⵉⵢⵓ ⴳⵓⵓⵙⴽⵓⵓ ⴳⵓⵏ ⴳⵓⵙⴽⴰ ⴰⵢⵓ.
Kekkuu goon kekka diyo gooskuu goon goska aanyo.
The resentful person died resentfully, the bon vivant lived.

> [Advice to be humble, not to be arrogant.]

---

35 *Hyphaene thebaica*, with common names dom palm and gingerbread tree, is a type of palm tree with edible oval fruit. It is a native to the Arabian Peninsula and also to the northern half of Africa where it is widely distributed and tends to grow in places where groundwater is present.

(357)

ⲱⲉⲕⲟⲛ ⲓⲙⲓⲗⲉⲕⲁ ⲕⲟⲫⲫⲓ ⲓⲙⲓⲗⲕⲟⲛ ⲱⲉⲕⲁ ⲕⲟⲫⲫⲓⲙⲟⲩⲛ.
Weekoon imileeka koffi imilkoon weeka koffimun.
One is like a hundred and a hundred is not equal to one.

[Said when missing someone valuable in a particular situation.]

(358)

ⲁⲇⲟⲩⲣⲣⲉⲗ ⲧⲟⲛ ⲧⲟⲣⲉ ⲫⲁⲙⲙⲟⲩⲛ.
Aburreel toon tooree fammun.
An axle is not made from the senna plant.[36]

[Said about someone who is capable of doing a certain task.]

(359)

ⲉⲇⲇⲓ ⲙⲉⲣⲁⲫⲓⲗⲅⲟⲛ ⲇⲟⲣⲣⲁ ⲟⲇⲓⲙⲟⲩⲛ.
Eddi merafiilgoon jorra odimun.
He does not urinate on his wounded hand.[37]

[Said about someone stingy.]

(360)

ⲛⲁϭϭⲓⲛ ⲁⲙⲁⲛⲛⲟⲅ ⲅⲓⲣⲃⲁⲛ ⲁⲙⲁⲛⲅⲁ ⲫⲟⲅⲁϭϭⲟ.
Naccin amannog girban amannga foogacco.
Through the water of the mirage, the jug spilled the water.

[Said when someone is losing what they already have by pursuing an illusion.]

---

36 *Cassia acutifolia*, known for its weak fibres.
37 Urine was used to cleanse some wounds in old Nubia.

(361)

ⲁï ⲦⲀⲚⲄⲀ ⲒⲢⲄⲞⲨⲘⲘⲞⲨⲚⲒ ⲔⲀⲆⲒⲚ ⲦⲀⲚⲚⲈⲤⲤⲀ.
Ay tannga irbummuuni kajin tannessa.
The one who does not know themself is more like a donkey.

[Said about somoene ignorant.]

(362)

ⲀⲆⲖⲒⲤⲈⲚ ⲒⲄⲞⲚ: ⲀⲰⲀⲚ ⲔⲞⲘⲘⲈⲚⲔⲀⲚ ⲞⲨⲄⲢⲈⲤⲔⲀ ⲤⲞⲨⲔⲔ ⲀⲘⲀⲚⲄⲀ ⲪⲀ ⲚⲒⲤⲈ ϳⲞⲚ.
Abliseen iigon: awaan kommeenkan ugreeska sukk amannga fa niise yon.
The fox said: If it had not been time, I would go out during the day and drink water.

[Said about someone who is very careful and suspicious.]

(363)

ⲀⲨⲀⲄ ⲌⲀⲘⲒⲆⲀⲖⲞⲄ ⲰⲒⲤⲔⲒⲢⲞⲚ.
Aashag hamiidalog wiskiron
He replaced Aisha with Hamida.

[Said when someone covets something from someone that no one else has.]

(364)

ⲦⲒⲚ ⲤⲞⲨⲄⲀ ⲀⲆⲀⲖⲒⲚ ⲤⲞⲨⲖⲞⲄ ⲰⲒⲤⲔⲒⲢⲞⲚ.
Tiin suuga abadin suulog wiskiron.
He exchanged cow milk with the sap of the apple of Sodom.[38]

[Said when someone exchanges something of good quality for something useless.]

---

38 The green fruits of the *Calotropis procera* contain a toxic milky sap that is extremely bitter and turns into a gluey coating which is resistant to soap. When we were kids, adults used to warn us about its danger, as we fondly picked the oval fruits of this plant, which resemble mangoes and playing with it like a ball.

(365)

ⲁⲩⲙⲁ̄ⲛ ⲓ̄ⲅ ⲕⲁⲗⲁⲅⲁ.
Ashmaan iig kalaga.
Like fire burning in the palm fibers.[39]

[Said about burning enthusiasm that soon subsides.]

(366)

ⲁ̄ⲇⲉⲙ ⲓⲛⲛⲓ ⲧⲁ̄ ⲓⲛⲛⲓⲗⲓⲛ.
Aadem inni taa innilin.
Whatever happens, your people are your people.

[Advice about the strength of kinship and family bonds.]

(367)

ⲁ̄ⲇⲉⲙⲓⲡⲓ̄ⲛⲁⲛ ⲃⲁⲩⲯⲓⲇⲧⲁ ⳝⲁ̄ⲅⲙⲟ̄ⲩⲛⲓ ⲛⲟ̄ⲣⲕⲁ ⳝⲁ̄ⲅⲙⲟⲩⲛⲛⲁ.
Aademiriinan banynyidta jaagmuuni noorka jaagmunna.
He who doesn't fear people's words, doesn't fear God.

[He who does not care about what people say and continues to do bad things.]

(368)

ⲁ̄ⲇⲉⲙⲓⲡⲓ̄ⲛ ⲙⲁ̄ⲯ ⲕⲓⲇⲧⲁ ⲕⲟⲣⳝⲉ̄ⲛ.
Aademiriin maany kidta korjeen.
The eyes of people crumble the rock.

[Advice about avoiding envy/evil eye of other people.]

---

39 Palm fibers have a quick fire and quick fade out.

(369)

ⲁⲇⲓ ⲉⲗⲉⲗⲁⲛ ⲕⲁⲇ̂ ⲫⲉⲛⲧⲓⲗ ⲇⲁⲣⲣⲟ̄ⲥⲟⲛ.
Adi eleelan kaj fentil darroocon.
Finally, the donkey has climbed palm tree.

> [When something impossible has happened.]

(370)

ⲁϳⲓⲛ ⲧⲟ̄ⲩⲃⲉⲛ ⲁⲅⲁⲣⲣⲁ ⲓⲣ ⲕⲓⲇⲇⲓⲛⲁⲙ.
Ayin tuuben agarra ir kiddinam.
What I wade into, you drown in.

> [Said when what I can do easily and simply exhausts you.]

(371)

ⲇⲓϳⲟ ⲫⲁ̄ⲣⲕⲁⲛ ⲁ̄ⲅ ⲧⲁⲫⲫⲓ̂ⲇⲓⲛ.
Diyo faarkan aag taffijin.
He comforts the deceased after his bones are worn out.

> [Said when a person talks about an issue when it's too late, or appropriates the pride and glories of his predecessors.]

(372)

ⲁ̄ⲅⲁ ⲛⲉⲇⲙⲉ̄ ⲗⲉⲕⲓⲛ ⲁ̄ⲱⲁ ⲛⲉⲇⲙⲉ̄ ⲅⲉⲛⲁ.
Aaga nedmee lekin Aawa nedmee gena.
It is better to regret what you did, than what you did not.

> [Advice for those who hesitate, as well as to relieve those who regret doing things and have not get what is hoped.]

(373)

ⲀⲄ ⲦⲀⲚⲄⲀ ⲘⲞⲨⲢⲦⲞⲨⲘⲞⲨⲚ.
Ag tannga murtumun.
He cannot control his mouth.

> [Said to excuse or blame someone who said something wrong.]

(374)

ⲀⲖⲈⲄ ⳄⲀⲨⲰⲞⲤⲀ ⲘⲒⲢⲀ ⲚⲀⳘ.
Aleeg banynyoosa mira naaf.
Say the truth and run.

> [Advice to tell the truth.]

(375)

ⲰⲈⲚⲀⲚ ⲆⲈⲄⲒⲆⲀ ⲘⲈⲚⲚⲀ.
Weenaan deegida menna.
They've been watered at the same time.

> [Said about the similarity between two or more people.]

(376)

ⲀⲖⲒ ⲀⲄⲄⲀⲚⲀⲚ ⲈⲰⲒⲦⲦⲒ ⲦⲈⲘⲈⲔⲔⲞⲨⲚⲀⲚ ⲚⲀⲖⲦⲒⲄⲞⲚ ⲞⲨ ⲘⲒⲢⲞⲆⲞⲚ.
Alii angnganaan ewetti temekkuunan naltigoon uu miiroojon.
My son Ali's (failed) cultivation prevented us even from seeing our neighbors.

> [Said about someone who is useless.]

(377)

ⲁⲗⲓ ⲉⲱⲣⲁⲧⲧⲁ ϳⲓⲕⲕⲁⲛ ⲧⲁⲛⲛⲉ̄ⲛ ⲛⲟ̄ⲅⲕⲁ ⳝⲁ ⲙⲓⲇⲇⲓⲕⲉ̄ⲛ.
Alii ewratta yikkan tanneen noogka fa middikeen.
If Ali were a good farmer, he would fill his mother's house (with good things).

> [Said sarcastically to someone who is useless.]

(378)

ⲁⲙⲁⲛ ⲥⲓ̄ⲧⲧⲓⲛ ⲧⲁⲱⲱⲟ ⲅⲟ̄ⲛ ⲇⲟⲱⲱⲓⲛ.
Aman siitin tawwo goon dowwin.
Water sneaking under the haystack.

> [Said to warn of the danger of a person or thing.]

(379)

ⲁⲙⲁⲛⲅⲟ̄ⲛ ⲉⲛⲛⲁ ⲁⲣⲣⲟⲩⲙⲟⲩⲛⲛⲁ.
Amangoon enna arrumunna.
He won't bring you water.

> [Said about a useless man.]

(380)

ⲁⲙⲃⲓⲅ ⲕⲟⲕⲕⲓ ⲁϳⲉⲣ ⲧⲁⲛⲅⲁ ⲛⲁⲙⲙⲟⲩⲛⲛⲁ.
Ambig kokki ayer tanga nammunna.
He who plants a dom palm tree will not see its fruits.

> [Said about someone who starts work that will take a long time.]

(381)

ⲁⲛⲛⲁⲱ ⲕⲟⲕⲕⲁ ⲙⲁⲱⲁⲗⲗⲁ ⲁⲅⲓⲛ.
Annaaw kokka mashalla aagin.
My grandmother sits alone in the sun.[40]

[Said about a stubborn person who insists on their opinion.]

(382)

ⲁⲛⲛⲉⲅⲁⲓ̈ ⲟⲩ̄ⲥⲕⲁ ⲟⲅⲟ̄ⲣⲁ ⲙⲁⲥⲕⲁ ⲇⲉⲗⲗⲓⲛ.
Annengayi uuska ogoora maska gillin.
My brother forgets the bad and remembers the good.

[Describes the characteristics of a loyal friend.]

(383)

ⲁⲣⲁⲇⲁ ⲱⲉ̄ⲗⲁ ⲇⲁⲙⲙⲁ ⲥⲓ̄ⲃⲃⲁ ⲟⲩⲇⲉ̄ⲛⲁ.
Arada weela jamma siicca udeena.
Have the shits in the same place.

[Said about a group when they agree on the same (bad) opinion.]

(384)

ⲁⲣⲓⲇⲇⲁ ⲓⲣⲃⲟⲩⲙⲙⲟⲩⲛⲓⲕⲕⲁ ⳍⲁⲙⲙⲁ̄ⲙⲓⲛ ⲟⲩⲥⲟⲩⲣⲕⲁ ⲧⲉ̄ⲛⲁ.
Arijca irbummunikka hammamn usurka teena.
Give the one who does not know meat pigeon's ass.

[Said about someone who is ignorant.]

---

40 This is also one of the riddles circulating in the Nubian regions, and its answer is ⲕⲟⲇⲓⲣ "stick to demarcate land and tie boats/animals to it."

(385)

ⲁⲣⲓⳝⳝⲁ ⲕⲁⲃⳝⲁ ⲅⲓⲥⲓⲣⲕⲁ ⲱⲓⲣⲕⲟⲛ.
Arijca kabja gisirka wirkon.
He ate the meat and threw the bone.

[Said about a selfish person.]

(386)

ⲁⲣⲓⳝⳝⲁ ⲥⲟⲩⲛⲛⲁ ⲙⲁ̄ⲣⲟⲗⲗⲉ̄ ⲙⲁⲣⲁⲅⲕⲁ ⲥⲉ̄ⲫⲓⲛ.
Arijca sunna marollee maragka seefin.
He who loses the meat eats the soup.

[Two meanings: advice about being content; said to ridicule people without initiative or diligence who are satisfied with little.]

(387)

ⲁⲣⳝⲉ̄ⲗⲁ ⲥⲉ̄ⲣⲣⲓ ⲇⲁ̄ⲫⲫⲓⲛ.
Arjeela seerri daafin.
There is gravel in the *arjee*.[41]

[Said when encountering an unwanted person or when something cannot be avoided.]

(388)

ⲁⲥⲥⲁⲣ ⳝⲁ̄ⲍⲓⳜ ⲙⲁⳜⲁⲣⲁ.
Assar shaahid madara.
The child is an acceptable witness.

[Advice that a child's testimony is credible.]

---

41 *Arjee* is a traditional Nubian dish, consisting of boiled beans or grains with added salt and cumin.

(389)

ⲁⲥⲥⲁⲣ ⲧⲁ̄ ⲕⲁⲙⲁⲅ̄ ⲕⲁⲛⲅ̄ⲟ̄ⲛ ⲁⲥⲥⲁⲣⲁ.
Assar taa kamang kangoon Assara.
A child, even if it becomes (the size of) a camel, is a child.

> [Advice that children remain children in their parents eyes, regardless of size, age, or social status.]

(390)

ⲁⲥⲥⲁⲣⲓ̄ⲇⲁⲛ ⲉⲱⲓⲣⲟⲗⲗⲟⲛ ⲟⲩⲓⲛ ⳤⲁⲙⲓ̄ⲣⲕ ⲉⲱⲓⲣⲁⲙ.
Assariidan ewirllon onyin hamiirk ewiram.
Who sowed with children, sowed cursed yeast.

> [Said when a person is forced to deal or partner with someone else who is not responsible.]

(391)

ⲁⲥⲥⲁⲣⲓ̄ⲛⲁⲛ ⲟⲩⲥⲟⲩⲣⲣⲁ ⲓ̄ⲅ ⲟⲩⲣⲣⲁ ⲇⲁ̄ⲫⲓ̄ⲛ.
Assariinan ussurra iig urra daafiin.
There is a burning flame in a child's ass.

> [Said about the hyperactivity of children.]

(392)

ⲁⲥⲥⲁⲣⲕⲁ ⲓⲕⲕⲁ ⲟⲩⲕⲟⲩⲙⲙⲟ̄ⲩⲛⲓⲛ ⲟⲩⲕⲓⲣ.
Assarka ikka onykummuunin onykir.
Make your child cry, before he makes you cry.

> [Advice to chastise your child, before they make you cry with their disobedience.]

(393)

ᴀccᴀpκᴀ Ⴠōჯɪɴɴᴀɴ cēpκᴀ κopмɪɴɴᴀᴄ̄ ᴀʌᴀᴦᴀ.
Assarka doonyinan seerka korminnang alaga.
Raising a child is like eating gravel.

> [Advice about how difficult it is to raise children.]

(394)

ᴀᴄ̄ɪccɪɴᴀɴ κoyᏏpeɴ ᴀᴦᴀppᴀ ᴀмᴀɴᴄ̄ᴀ ɴīтᴀм.
Angissinan kubren agarra amannga niitam.
Do not drink water where the fish are disturbed.

> [Advice not to drink at a spot where the fish are scared, their abnormal movement indicating a risk in water.]

(395)

ᏴᴀჯჯɪႠ Ⴠoyκκɪ ႠoʌʌɪκκᴀɪpᏏɪммoyɴɴᴀ.
Banynyid dukki dollika irbimmunna.
Speech does not know a deep mound.

> [Said to someone who speaks with a double tongue.]

(396)

ᏴᴀჯჯɪႠ ōjᴦᴀ тɪᴦɪɴɴᴀᴄ̄ᴀ ᴀʌᴀᴦᴀ.
Banynyid ooyga tiginnanga alaga.
Speech is like tracking someone's feet.

> [Said about someone who is trying to drag out information or thoughts from someone.]

(397)

ᏴᴀჯჯɪႠтᴀ ẟᴀᴦɪκκᴀ ᏴᴀჯჯɪႠ ʌepᴦɪɴ.
Banynyidta jaagikka banynyid lergin.
Words follow those who are afraid of it.

> [Said to induce courage.]

(398)

Ⲃⲁⲛⲛⲓⲇⲧⲁ ⲱⲁⲓⲁⲫⲓⲛ ⲁⲫⲫⲓⲙⲓⲛⲓ ⲅⲟⲩⲇⲇⲟ ⲛⲁⲇⲇⲟⲕⲁⲛ ⲁⲫⲫⲟⲩⲙⲟⲩⲛⲛⲁ.
Banynyidta waayafiin affimiini guddo naddookan affumunna.
He who does not pick the words while they are in the air, will not catch them after they falls to the ground.

[Advice about the importance of intuition and a quick mind.]

(399)

Ⲃⲁⲛⲛⲓⲇ ⲧⲁⲛ ⲅⲟⲩⲇⲇⲟ ⲛⲁⲇⲇⲟⲩⲙⲟⲩⲛ.
Banynyid tan guddo naddumun.
His words do not fall to the ground.

[Two meanings: said about a person who is commanding and obeyed among his people; said about an envious person who harms people and their property, so people fear of them.]

(400)

Ⲃⲁⲛⲛⲓⲇ ⲧⲁⲛⲛⲓ ⲕⲁⲛⲇⲓ ⲅⲁⲗⲁⲅⲁ(ⲕⲁⲛⲇⲁ).
Banynyid tanni kandi galaga (kanda).
His words are (sharp) like a knife.

[Said about the person who is strict and sharp with his words.]

(401)

Ⲃⲉⲇⲣⲓ ⲓⲟⲩⲛⲛⲓ ⲕⲟⲩⲣⲕⲟⲩⲣⲁⲡⲟⲩⲛⲁⲛ Ⲃⲉⲇⲣⲓⲓⲁ.
Bedri yunni kurkuraabuunan bedriya.
As early as the people of Naga kurkur's early.[42]

[Said about someone breaking promises.]

---

[42] Proverb used in the villages of Aniba and Tōmās wa Afye. The people of Nag (Karkar) of Tōmās wa Afye used to go to the lands of the neighboring village Aniba, and whenever they promised to go early in the next day, they broke their promise.

(402)

Ƃoypōyг oyλoyмnān aгιλaгōn ωιpк oyΔιp.
Buruug ulumnaan agilagoon wirk udir.
Throw the girl even if it is the mouth of a crocodile.

[Advice to let a daughter marry quickly
when the time has come.]

(403)

Ƃoypōy ιмīΔιn гapāpa.
Buruu imiidin garaara.
A girl is like a bag of salt.

[Advice to let a daughter marry quickly
when the time has come.]

(404)

ωēтānīnān Фoгocca мeccīnna ōy каωωējа мecco.
Sheetaaniinaan fongossa messiina uu kashsheeya messo.
When the demons were buds, we were fruits.

[Said about experience and old age.]

(405)

ωēтānīnān δaммen aгappa ιδλīc δōy.
Sheetaaniinan jammen agarra ibliis juu.
Satan goes to the place where the demons gather.

[Said to express a group having many
(esp. bad) things in common.]

(406)

ⲰⲈ̄ⲦⲀⲚⲒ̄ⲚⲀⲚ ⲔⲒⲦⲦⲒⲄ ⲔⲒ̄ⲆⲀⳐⲒ̄Ⲛ.
Sheetaaniinan kittig kiidafiin.
Wearing a demon's dress.

[Said about a deceitful, broad-minded, and resourceful person.]

(407)

ⲰⲈ̄ⲒⲄⲞ̄Ⲛ ⲦⲀⳌⲢⲀⲄⲞ̄ⲨⲖⲞⲄⲞⲰⲀ ⳌⲈ̄ⲂⲀⲄⲞ̄Ⲛ ⳐⲀ̄ⲦⲘⲀ ⲄⲀⲢⲢⲒⲄⲞ̄ⲨⲖⲞⲄⲞⲰⲀ.
Sheeyigoon tahraguulogowa heebagoon faatma garriguulogowa.
Wealth through Tahra's lucky family, prestige through Fatma's unlucky family.

[Said when comparing between lucky and unlucky.]

(408)

ⲔⲀⲆⳆⲀ ⲆⲞ̄ⲄⲒⲚⲀⲚ ⲰⲀⲄⲦⲒⲄⲀ ⲀⲖⲞ̄ⲨⲄⲔⲀ ⲦⲈ̄ⲚⲀ?
Kajca dooginan wagtiga aluugka teena?
Are they going to feed donkeys while they are riding?

[Said when doing things at an inappropriate time.]

(409)

ⳐⲒⲖⲀ̄Ⲛ ⳆⲒⲘⲘⲈ̄Ⳉ ⲚⲀⲔⲒⲦⲦⲀⲚ ⲰⲒ̄ⲢⲒ ⲰⲒ̄ⲢⲒⲔⲔⲀ ⲚⲞ̄ⲨⲢⲀⲔⲈ̄.
Filaan jimmeez nakiitan wiiri wiirikka nuurakee.
Like a sycamore tree, its shadow extends to those who are not sitting under it.

[Said about someone who looks after or serves other people than his family or relatives.]

(410)

ⲱⲁ̄ⲣⲧⲓⲛ ⲱⲁⲕⲕⲓⲥⲓ̄ⲛ Δⲓ̄ⲥ ⲫⲟ̄ⲅⲕⲟⲩⲙⲙⲟ.
Shaartin shakkisiin diis foogkummo.
He was stabbed with a spear and did not bleed.

> [Said when a person hears something that requires a response, intervention, or comment but does not utter a word.]

(411)

ⲱⲓϐⲓⲣ ⲟⲩⲕⲕⲓⲗⲟⲅ ⲟⲩⲱⲱⲟ ⲉⲛⲛⲓⲛⲛⲁ.
Shibir ukkilog uwwo enninna.
The two-handled basket is held by two people.

> [Said about collaboration on assignments or work.]

(412)

ⲱⲓϐⲓⲣⲓⲛ ⲟⲩⲫⲫⲓⲗⲟⲅ ⲛⲁΔΔⲟ̄ⲥⲟⲛ.
Shibirin uffilog naddooson.
He fell out of the basket's hole.

> [Said when ignoring, forgetting, or belittling someone.]

(413)

ⲱⲓϐⲓⲣⲣⲁ ⲟⲩⲕⲕⲓ ⲙⲉⲛδⲓⲛ.
Shibirra ukki menjin.
A basket has handles.

> [Said to warn against eavesdroppers.]

(414)

ⲱⲟ̄ⲃⲁⲛ ⲇⲁⲅⲇⲁⲅⲓⲗⲁ ⲧⲟ̄ⲣⲟⲛ.
Shooban dangdangila tooron.
He got lost in a long time ago.

[Said of someone who is out of sight, when someone unwanted has disappeared.]

(415)

ⲱⲟ̄ⲣⲧⲓ ⲧⲁⲛ ⲧⲓⲥⲥⲓⲛⲁⲛ ⲇ̄ⲟⲩⲇⲉϳⲁ.
Shoorti tan tissinan juudeya.
A calm, peaceful-minded spirit.

[Said in praise of a patient person.]

(416)

ⲱⲟⲅⲅⲓⲣⲕⲟ̄ⲛ ⲱⲟⲅⲅⲓⲣⲕ ⲉⲣⲅⲓⲛ.
Shongngirkoon shongngirk ergin.
Money follows money.

[Two meanings: said to denote livelihood and large amounts of money; said to console the poor for their lack of money.]

(417)

ⲇⲁϩⲁ̄ⲛ ⲁ̄ⲧⲉ̄ ⲧⲁⲕⲕⲁ ⲁⲥⲣⲓⲛ ⲁ̄ⲧⲉ̄ⲅ ⲇⲟⲩⲱⲱⲓ ⲕⲓⲙⲙⲟⲩⲛⲛⲁ.
Dahaan aatee takka asrin aateeg duwwi kimmunna.
The shadow of the forenoon will not take him to the shadow of the afternoon.

[Said about someone who is hesitant but needs to switch gears.]

(418)

ⲇoyⲛjⲁ ⲇⲁⳅⲁⲛ ⲁ̄ⲧⲉ̄ⲅ ⲁⲗⲁⲅⲁ.
Dunya dahaan aateeg alaga.
Life is like the shadow of forenoon.

[Advice that life is finite.]

(419)

ⲁⲥⲣⲓⲛ ⲙⲁⲱⳃⲁ ⲉⲇⲉ̄ⲛ ⲇⲟ̄ⲱⲕⲁ ⲇⲟ̄ⲱⲕⲉ̄ⲛ.
Asrin masha edeen dooshka dooshkeen.
The afternoon sun tricks only the stupid woman.

[Advice to get our work done on time.]

(420)

ⲇⲁⲫⲫⲟ ⲧⲁ ⲇⲁⲫⲫⲟⲗⲗⲓⲛⲛⲁ.
Daffo ta daffollinna.
What is lost has been lost.

[Said to console someone for what they lost, if they are sure that it cannot be found.]

(421)

ⲇⲁ̄ⲣⲓⲕⲕⲁ ⲉⲛⲛⲓⲛⲁⲛ oyⲕⲕⲟ̄ⲛ ⲅoyⲥⲥⲉ̄ⲛ oyⲥoyⲣⲕⲁ ⲧⲟ̄jⲓⲛ oyⲕⲕⲟ̄ⲛⳝⲁ ⲕⲓⲕⲕⲓⲕⲓⲣ.
Daarikka enninan ukkoon gusseeen usurka tooyin ukkoonga kikkikir.
Make the day of harvest and day of storage barn cleanliness the same day.

[Advice to farmers to organize their work well.]

(422)

ⲆⲀⲰⲰⲒⲚⲀⲚ ⲒⲆⲀ ϫⲒⲙⲙⲟⲨⲚⲚⲀ.
Dawwinan ida yimmun.
He is not a man of the road.

[Said about anyone who cannot be taken as a travel companion.]

(423)

Ⲇⲉⲯⲯⲁ̄ⲣⲁ ⲧⲟ̄ⲩ̄ⲡ/ⲅⲟ̄ⲩ̄ⲡ ⲙⲟⲩⲛⲛⲁ.
Denynyaara tuup/guup munna.
The prostitute does not regret/deny.

[Said about someone who does not admit, regret, or repent for their wrongdoing.]

(424)

ⲆⲒϳⲀⲪⲒ̄ⲚⲦⲀ̄Ⲛ ⲔⲞⲪⲪⲀ ⲪⲒ̄ ⲘⲞⲨⲚⲚⲀ.
Diyafiintaan koffa fii munna.
Even though he's dead, he's not covered (does not find a grave).

[Said about a useless person.]

(425)

ⲆⲒⲆ ⲚⲞⲨⲖⲞ̄ⲨⲚⲀⲚ ⲞⲨⲚⲚⲀ̄ⲆⲀ.
Dib nuluunan unnaada.
Born on a white night.

[Said when being optimistic about the goodness of a person.]

(426)

ⲆⲒⲢⲂⲀⲆⲞⲚⲆⲒ ⲄⲈⲘⲈ̄ⲖⲀ ⲔⲞⲨⲘⲂⲞⲨ ⲰⲈ̄ⲔⲀ ⲞⲨⲚⲚⲒⲚ ⲚⲀⲔⲒⲦⲦⲀⲚ.
Dirbadondi gemeela kumbu weeka unnin nakittan.
As if the rooster lays an egg a year.

[Said about someone who claims to be what they are not.]

(427)

Ⲇⲟⲩⳇⲛⲁⲛ Ⳓⲁⲡⲡⲉⲕⲕⲁ ⲟⲩⲛⲉ̄ⲕⲟ̄ Ⲇⲟⲩⲙⲙⲓⲛ.
Dooshiinan banynyekka uneekoo duummin.
What the idiot says is understood by the sane.

> [Advice that wisdom may be pronounced by insane people, and the sane person should pay attention to what they say.]

(428)

Ⲇⲟⲅⲉ̄ ⲕⲉⲛⲧⲓ Ⲧⲁⲛⲛⲁ ⳝⲟⲩ̄ ⲛⲟⲩⲱⲩⲱⲓⲛ.
Dogee kenti tanna juu nuwwin.
The dove goes to sleep in its nest.

> [Said to induce bonding and to be at home.]

(429)

Ⲫⲉⲇⲇⲉⲕⲕⲓⲣⲁ ⲗⲉ̄ Ⲫⲉⲇⲇⲉⲛ Ⳓⲁⲗⲉ̄ⲅ ⲁ̄ⲱⲱⲁ?
Feddekkira lee fedden baleeg aawwa?
Are we borrowing and holding a wedding with borrowed money?

> [Advice only to borrow money for emergencies.]

(430)

Ⲇⲟ̄ⲣⲟⲛ ⲅⲁ̄ⲇⲓ̄ Ⲫⲁ̄ⳇⲉⲕⲕⲁ Ⲧⲁⲱⲱⲟⲛ ⲅⲁ̄ⲇⲓ̄ Ⲫⲁ̄ⳇⲓⲛ/Ⲧⲁⲡⲡⲓⲕⲉ.
Dooron gaadii faayekka tawwon gaadii faayin/tanynyike.
What the upper judge[43] writes, is written/approved by the lower judge.

> [Advice to have faith in God and his will.]

---

43 I.e., God.

(431)

ⲉⲥⲕⲓ ⲁ̄ⲱⲓⲛ ⲫⲉ̄ⲱⲓⲛ.
Eski aawin feewin.
Those who are able do and solve.

> [Said about a skilled person exercising their profession.]

(432)

ⲉⲇⲇⲓ ⲧⲁⲛⲛⲟⲅ ⲕⲁⲃⲓ ⲁⳝⲧⲁⲛⲅⲁ ⲉⲛⲛⲓⲛ.
Eddi tannog kabi aytanga ennin.
He who eats with his hand strengthens himself.

> [Advice to do what is good for you.]

(433)

ⲕⲟ̄ⲛⲁⲛ ⲟⲩⲛⲛⲓⲥⲓ̄ⲛ ⲇⲓⲃⲗⲁ ⲟⲩⲛⲛⲁⲫⲓ̄ⲛ.
Koonan unnisiin dibla unnafiin.
He has been born on the night that crescent appeared.

> [A blessing given on the birthday of a beloved one.]

(434)

ⲉⲥⲕⲓ ⲙⲓⲛⲅⲁ ⲙⲉⲥⲕⲓ.
Eski minga meski.
A skilled person can do anything.

> [Said about a person who can fulfill their desires by all means because of their skilfulness.]

(435)

ⲉⲇⲇⲓ ⲱⲉ̄ⲗⲉⲕⲓⲛ ⲟⲩⲱⲱⲟ ⲅⲉⲛⲁ ⲟⲩⲱⲱⲟ ⲗⲉⲕⲓⲛⲅⲟ̄ⲛ ⲧⲟⲩⲥⲕⲟ ⲅⲉⲛⲁ.
Eddi weelekin uwwo gena uwwo lekingoon tusko gena.
Two hands are better than one, three better than two.

> [Advice about the advantage of cooperation.]

(436)

ⲉⲅⲉⲇⲓⲛ ⲕⲉⲣⲃⲉⲕⲕⲁ ⲕⲁⲧⲧⲓ ⲉⲧⲓⲙ ⲱⲉⲗⲁ ⲕⲟⲩⲗⲗⲓⲛ.
Egedin kerbekka katti etiim weela kullin
He learns to shear a sheep with an orphan lamb.

> [Said about professionals who are unskilled at their work or do a bad job on purpose.]

(437)

ⲉⲅⲉⲇ ⲉⲅⲉⲇⲓⲇⲇⲁⲛ ϫⲁⲙⲙⲁ ⲫⲁⲅ ⲫⲁⲅⲓⲇⲇⲁⲛ ϫⲁⲙⲙⲓⲛ.
Eged egediddan jamma fag fagiddan jammin.
Sheep meets with sheep, goats meet with goat.

> [Advice that each is looking for his companion.]

(438)

ⲉⲗⲉ ϫⲉⲛⲃⲁⲗ ⲓⲣ ⲓⲇⲇⲁⲅⲟⲟⲥ.
Ele jenbal ir iddangoos.
O, side piece of the garment, be the sleeve.

> [Said about someone demanding a role or stature that is not appropriate for him.]

(439)

ⲉⲗⲓⲓⲛⲁⲁⲛ ⲕⲟⲩⲙⲃⲟⲩ ⲱⲁⲗⲗⲟⲛ ⲇⲓⲣⲃⲁⲇⲁ.
Eliinaan kumbu wallon dirbada.
Today's egg is tomorrow's hen.

> [Advice not to underestimate children, but strengthen their confidence and treat them as responsible adults.]

(440)

ⲕⲟⲣⲉ̄ⲗⲁ ⲕⲟ̄ⲥⲣⲟⲩⲇⲟ ⲕⲟⲣⲉ̄ⲗⲁ ⲕⲟ̄ⲥⲟⲩⲣ.
Koreela koosrudo koreela koosur.
Since we got full at the (last) feast, we get full at the (next) feast.

[Said when postposing to buy something until it becomes necessary.]

(441)

ⲉⲣⲉ̇ⲓ̈ ⲓ̇ⲓⲥⲥ ⲁ̄ⲇⲓ⳵ ⲙⲓⲇⲣⲉ̄ ⲅⲓⲧⲧⲓⲕⲕ ⲉⲛⲛⲓⲛ.
erey yiss aajiz midree gittikk ennin.
The lazy captain carries a heavy pole.[44]

[Said about a lazy person.]

(442)

ⲉⲇⲇⲓ ⲱⲉ̄ ⲟⲗⲗⲓⲅ ⲟⲩϣⲓⲙⲙⲟⲩⲛ.
Eddi wee ollig ushimmun.
One hand does not clap.

[Advice to encourage cooperation.]

(443)

ⲇⲟⲩⲅⲅⲓ ⲙⲓⲛⲅⲁ ⲉⲗⲟ? ⲙⲁ̄ⲛ̇ⲓⲗⲧⲟ̄ⲛ ϣⲓⲃⲓⲣⲱⲉ̄ⲕⲕⲁ.
Dungngi minnga elo? Maanyiltoon shibirweekka.
What did the blind find? A basket of eyes.

[Said when you unexpectedly find what you really wanted.]

---

44 A wooden tool/pole for measuring the depth of water.

(444)

ⲉⲥⲕⲓ ⲕⲁⲩϳⲓⲛ ⲕⲁⲃⲓⲛ ⲙⲟⲗⲗⲁ ⲅⲟⲛ ⲇⲓⲇⲉⲗⲟⲅ ⲁⲣϫⲉⲅ ⲟⲕⲕⲉⲛ.
Eski kaashin kaabin moolla goon diideelog arjeeg okkeen.
The masters can cook, knead, and boil the grains at the same time.

[Said about a skilled person.]

(445)

Ⲫⲉⲗⲗⲁ ⲧⲟⲣⲟ Ⲫⲉⲗⲗⲁ Ⲫⲁⲙⲙⲟⲩⲛⲛⲁ.
Fedda tooro fedda fammunna.
The thing that came by begging cannot be taken out by begging.

[Advice to warn someone who is in a rush.]

(446)

Ⲇⲟⲅⲉⲛ ⲟⲩⲡⲡⲁⲅⲟⲛ ⲱⲉ ⲙⲉⲛⲇⲓⲛ ⲧⲁⲕⲕⲁ Ⲃⲓⲅⲇⲓⲛ ⲟⲩⲡⲡⲁⲅⲟⲛ ⲱⲉ ⲙⲓⲛⲇⲓⲛ.
Dogeen urragoon wee menjin takka bigdin urragoon wee minjin.
One stands to hunt the dove, and the other to hunt the hunter.

[Advice that someone who searches for others' mistakes will surely search for your mistakes too.]

(447)

Ⲫⲉⲛⲧⲓⲅ ⲕⲟⲩⲛⲉ ⲗⲉⲕⲓⲛ ⲟ̄ϳⲅⲁ ⲕⲟⲩⲛⲕⲁⲛ ⲅⲉⲛⲁ.
Fentig kunee lekin ooyga kunkan gena.
It is better to have your legs than to have a palm tree.

[Advice that when comparing the ownership of something with the ability to work, the harvester's share may exceed what the owners may get.[45]]

---

[45] The worker who harvested dates was taking a percentage of the crop to care for cleaning, fertilizing the palm throughout the year and harvesting the crop in the season.

(448)

Ⲫⲉⲗⲉⲕⲕⲁ ⲕⲁⲃⲁⲫⲓ̄ⲛ ⲧⲟ̄ⲩ ⲟⲣⲟⲙⲁⲫⲓ̄ⲛ.
Felekka kabafiin tuu oromafiin.
The stomach of someone who eat onion will be cold.

[Advice that the offender is betrayed by his actions.]

(449)

Ⲅⲁ̄ⲱⲁⲛⲇⲓⲅ ⲥⲓⲇⲇⲟ ⲫⲁ ⲇⲟ̂ⲩ ϫⲓⲥⲥⲁⲛ? ⲟⲩⲃⲟⲩⲣⲧⲓⲛⲁⲛ ⲇⲟⲩⲕⲕⲓⲗⲁⲓϳⲟⲛ.
Gaashandig siddo fa juu yissan? Uburtinan dukkilaiyon.
When they asked the show-off, 'Where are you going?' 'The ash mound.'

[Advice that beauty is useless without work and good manners.]

(450)

Ⲅⲉⲱϫⲓⲅ ⲓ̄ⲅⲗⲁ ⲇⲉⲧⲧⲁ ⲟⲩⲇⲉ̄ⲛ.
Geshig iigla detta udeen.
Gather dry weeds and throw them into the fire.

[Said about those who provoke and cause animosity among people.]

(451)

Ⲅⲓⲥⲓⲣ ⲕⲟⲣⲇ̂ⲁ ⲃⲁ̄ϳ ⲙⲟⲩⲛⲛⲁ.
Gisir korja baay munna.
The bone breaks but does not separate.

[Advice that kinship ties must not be separated, whatever happens.]

(452)

ⲅoyⲱⲱaⲛaⲛ ⲕaⲙⲅaⲗē ΔōⲅaΦı?
Guwwanan kamgalee doogafi?
Are you an ant camel rider?

> [Said about someone who walks very slow,
> as if riding a camel of ants.]

(453)

ZapāппōN ⲙōлa aⲙāⲣⲕōN ⲱīⲣa.
Harappoon moola amaarkoon wiira.
Destruction is near, while reconstruction is far.

> [Advice about the difficulty of building
> and easiness of sabotage.]

(454)

ıϬıp ⲙeⲛδıN ıϬıpıN ⲙōлⲕa ⱳāⲅıN.
Ibir menjin ibirin moolka shaagin.
While the target stays, he hits next to it.

> [Said when someone doesn't do/say what they
> were asked to do even though it was clear.]

(455)

ıϬoNeⲅⲅaN TōΔıNaN ⲕaNΔı ıⲕⲕa ⲅoδⲙoyN.
Ibonengngan toodinan kandi ikka gojmun.
Your cousin's knife does not slaughter you.

> [Advice that your family cannot harm you.]

(456)

ⲧⲓⲛⲟⲛ ⲧⲟⲇ ⲙⲁⲧⲧⲟⲛ ⲁⲥⲕⲁ ⲉⲇⲟⲛ.
Tinon tood matton aska edon.
A son of the east married to a daughter of the west.

> [Advice that marriage is pure luck, you can't know with whom, where, and how.]

(457)

ⲓⲇⲉⲛ ⲫⲁⲕⲕⲁⲛⲅⲟⲛ ⲙⲉⲣⲓⲛ ⲧⲟⲕⲕⲁⲛⲅⲟⲛ ⲙⲉⲣⲓⲛ.
Ideen fakkanngoon merin tookkanngoon merin.
When a woman goes out it cuts (has an effect), when she enters it cuts.

> [Said to mediate especially when marital problems occur.]

(458)

ⲓⲇⲓⲛⲛⲓⲛ ⲕⲁⲃⲁⲕⲕⲁ ⲇⲉⲥⲥⲁ ϳⲓⲛⲓⲛ ⲕⲁⲃ.
Idinnin kabakka dessa yinin kab.
Eat your husband's food, even if it's raw.

> [Advice for a wife to obey her husband, and to warn her for the consequences of not doing so, lest he marry someone else.]

(459)

ⲓⲇⲗⲟⲛ ⲃⲁⲍⲁⲣⲁ ϳⲓⲕⲕⲁⲛ ⲓⲇⲉⲛ ϻⲓⲥⲣⲁ.
Idlon bahara yikkan ideen jisra.
If the husband is a sea, then the wife is a bridge.

> [Advice about the harmony between husband and wife.]

(460)

ⲓⲕⲕⲁ ⲁⲣⲕⲓⲗⲟⲅ ⲟⲩⲩⲉ̄ⲕⲕⲁ ⲕⲓⲇⲓⲛⲁⲛ ⲕⲟⲣϫⲓⲇⲟⲗⲗⲟⲅ ⲟⲩⲩⲓⲣ.
Ikka arkilog usheekka kidinan korjidollog ushir.
Hit the one who hit you with mud with a stone.

> [Said when the response to an offense is stronger than the offense itself.]

(461)

ⲓⲕⲕⲁ ⲓⲣⲃⲟⲩⲙⲙⲟⲩⲛⲁⲛ ⲁⲅⲁⲣⲣⲁ ⲙⲉⲣⲅ̄ⲟⲥⲁ ⲁⲣⲁⲅ.
Ikka irbummunan agarra mergoosa arag.
In a place where no one knows you dance like crazy.

> [Advice to act freely as long as you are out of sight of those who may know you.]

(462)

ⲓⲕⲕⲁ ⲫⲉϫⲓⲣⲛⲁⲛ ⲉⲱⲱⲉⲗⲗⲟⲅ ⲧⲉ̄ⲛⲛⲁⳝⲁ ⲥⲁⲗⲁϫⲁ ϳⲓⲕⲕⲁⲛⳝⲟⲛ ⲙⲟ̄ⲛⲧⲁⲙ.
Ikka fejirnan ewwellog teenanga salaja yikkangoon moontam.
Do not refuse what they give you early in the morning, even if it is a kick.

> [Said to encourage early work and not to reject anything that comes in the morning, even if it's bad it may be a sign of much good.]

(463)

ⲓⲕⲕⲁ ⲙⲁ̄ⲯ ⲱⲉ̄ⲗⲗⲟⲅ ⳝⲟ̄ⲩⲯⲟⲕⲕⲁ ⲟⲩⲱⲱⲟⲗⲟⲅ ⳝⲟ̄ⲩⲯ.
Ikka maany weellog guunyokka uwwolog guuny.
He who looks at you with one eye, look at him with two.

> [Two meanings: advice to be good to those who are good to you and harm back those who harm you; to be better to someone who is good to you and to double down on abuse.]

(464)

ⲓⲕⲕⲁ ⲧⲉⲃⲃⲁϳⲁ ⲟⲩⲣ ⲓⲛⲅⲁ ⲉⲗⲓⲥ.
Ikka tebbaya ur innga elis.
I looked for you and found your head.

[Said when you miss a person dear to you.]

(465)

ⲓⲕⲕⲁ ⲧⲓⲥⲥⲓ ⲕⲟⲅⲟⲣⲟⲕⲕⲓ ⲗⲁⲅⲟ̄ⲛ ⲟ̄ϳⲓⲛⲅⲁ ⲧⲓⲅⲓⲛ.
Ikka tissi kogorokki lagoon oyinga tigin.
He who hates you tracks your footprints in the rocky land.

[Advice that someone who hates you will continue to look for any slip you make.]

(466)

ⲓⲕⲕⲁ ⲧⲓⲥⲥⲓ ⲓⲛⲥⲓⲣⲥⲟⲩⲕⲕⲉⲗⲗⲟⲅ ⲥⲓⲙⲁⲣⲕⲟⲩⲙⲟⲩⲛⲛⲁ.
Ikka tissi insirsukkellog simarkumunna.
He who hates you is not saddened by your slipping and falling.

[Advice about hatred and envy.]

(467)

ⲓⲛ ⲓⲣⲕⲓⲗ ⲙⲁⲱⲁⲛⲁⲛ ⲙⲉⲣⲉⲕⲕⲁ ⲧⲓ̄ⲅⲉϳⲁ ⲓ̄ⲅⲙⲟⲩⲛⲛⲁⲛ.
In irkil mashanan merekka tiigeya iigmunnan.
In this village they do not welcome the stranger after sunset.

[Said about miserliness.]

(468)

ᎢᎾᏙᏂ ᎤᏯᏍ ᎺᏕᎢᏁᎸ ᎤᏯᏌ.
Indon uus mediinel uusa.
A villain here is a villain anywhere.

> [Advice that a bad person may not change
> no matter where they go.]

(469)

ᎢᏁᎾᎦ ᎣᏯᏍᎩᏆ ᎠᏁᎾᎦ ᎡᏁᎴᎡ?
Ineenga uskir aneenga enneelee?
You take care of your mother, and neglect mine?!

> [Said about a selfish person who only considers his
> own interests and does not care about others.]

(470)

ᎢᏈᏂ ᎧᏆᏍᏇᏂᏃᏂ ᎢᎧᎧ ᎢᏌᏎᎦ.
Iriin kabsiinnon ikka issiga.
What you ate begs you.

> [Said to someone who ate in your house but turned against you.]

(471)

ᎢᏁᏂ ᎢᎧᎧ ᎠᏕᎠᏉᎠᎦ ᎠᏉᎠᏖᏁ.
Inni ikka adaawaga aawateen.
Your relative might be causing you enmity.

> [Advice about the problems that individuals
> may cause to their families and relatives.]

(472)

ⲓⲛⳝⲟ̄ⲛ ⲫⲁ̄ⲓ̇ⲁ ⲫⲓⲓ̇ⲟⲛⲧⲁ̄ⲛ ⲛⲁ̄ⲫⲁ ⲫⲓⲓ̇ⲟⲗⲗⲓⲛ.
Inngoon faaya fiyontaan naafa fiyollin.
Although this was written, it was hidden.

> [Said when something bad happens unexpectedly.]

(473)

ⲓⲣⲓ̄ⲛ ⳇⲁⲯⲯⲓⳅⲓ̄ⲛ ⲓⲕⲕⲁ ⲁⲗⲅⲓⲛ.
Iriin banynyisiin ikka algin.
What you said is like you.

> [Advice that what you say shows your true nature.]

(474)

ⲓⲗⲗⲓⲙ ⲧⲁ̄ ⲕⲉⲛ ⳜⲁⳡⳜⲁⳡⲓⲗⲗⲁ ⲧⲟ̄ⲣⲟ.
Illim taa ken dangdangilla tooro.
What is wrong with you to go to the wilderness?

> [Said about someone who disappears for a while and then returns.]

(475)

ⲓⲗⲗⲓⲙ ⲧⲁ̄ ⲕⲁⲙ ⲕⲟ̄ⲩⳝⲉ̄/Ⳝⲓⳝⲓⲛⲧⲉ̄ ⲗⲁⲧⲟ̄ⲛ ⲧⲟⲩⲣⲥⲁⲛⲁⲛ ⲁⲗⲁⳝⲁⳡⲟ.
Illim taa kam kuushee(digintee) latoon tursanan alagango.
Why did you become like camels expelled from a safflower/cowpea field?

> [Said when meeting a miserable or sad person.]

(476)

ⲓⲣ ⲧⲁ̄ ⲟⲩⲗⲟⲩⲙⲗⲓ ⲉⲛⲛⲟⲛ ⲧⲟ̄ⲣⲉ̄ⲅⲁ ⲱⲓⲣⲕⲁ ⲟⲩⲇ ⲓⲣⲥⲁⲛ ⲛⲉ̄?
Ir taa ulumli ennon tooreega wirka ud irsan nee?
Are you that eaten by the crocodile, and they threw the axle behind them and went?

> [Said about someone who was out of sight, then suddenly appears.]

(477)

ⲓⲧⲧⲓⲣ ⲟ̄ⲩ̄ⲥⲕⲁ ⲟⲕⲕⲉ̄ⲛ.
Ittir uuska okkeen.
She cooks a bad *ittir*.[46]

> [Said about someone with bad cooking skills or who cannot do even the easiest jobs.]

(478)

ⳝⲁ̄ϩⲁⲗ ⲁϊ ⲧⲁⲛⲛⲓⲛ ⲁⲇⲟⲩⲱⲱⲁ.
Jaahal ay tannin aduwwa.
The fool is the enemy of himself.

> [Said about someone ignorant.]

(479)

ⳝⲉⲗⲗⲓⲅⲁ ⲟⲅ ⲱⲉ̄ⲇⲟⲧⲟ̄ⲛ ⲁ̄ⲱⲁ ⲧⲁⲯⲉ.
Jelliga og weedotoon aawa tanynye.
Do your work from start to finish.

> [Advice to finish the work assigned to you.]

---

46 See fn. 13.

(480)

ⲇⲟⲩⲙⲉⲥⲥⲁⲛ ⲕⲟⲩⲗⲗⲁ ⲫⲁ ⲇⲟⲩⲛ.
Juumessan kulla fa juun.
He will go to the hole where no one has gone.

[Said when someone does something that they know has a bad ending.]

(481)

ⲕⲁⲃⲁⲫⲓ̄ ⲙⲓⲣⲓ̄ⲇ ⲱⲉ̄ⲗⲟⲛ ⲇⲁ̄ⲕⲕⲁⲛⲅⲟ̄ⲛ ⲙⲓⲣⲓⲛ.
Kabafii miriid weelon daakanngoon mirin.
The one whose eaten plenty runs if it's necessary to run.

[Advice to eat before leaving the house, just in case you're out of the whole day; also said to encourage guests to eat.]

(482)

ⲕⲁⲃⲁⲣ ⲓⲛⲛⲓⲅ ⲕⲁⲃⲟ̄ⲥⲟⲛ ⲛⲁⲣ ⲁⲛⲛⲓ ⲙⲉⲣⲟ̄ⲥⲟⲛ.
Kabar innig kabooson nar anni merooson.
I ate your food, and my tongue was cut off.

[Advice that who eats your food will not speak (bad) about you.]

(483)

ⲕⲁⲇϫⲁ ⲕⲟⲩⲛⲓ ⲟ̈ⲓ̈ⲗⲟⲅ ⲧⲁⲩⲯⲟⲩⲙⲟⲩⲛⲛⲁ.
Kajca kuni ooylog tanynymunna.
He who owns a donkey does not walk on his feet.

[Said about someone who is self-sufficient and doesn't need others.]

(484)

ⲕⲁⲧⲧⲓ ⲧⲁⲛⲛⲉ̄ⲛ ⲫⲁ̄ⲅⲕⲁ ⲧⲁⲗⲗⲓⲛ.
Katti tanneen faagka tallin.
The (wool of the) lamb looks like the wool of his mother.

[Said when a child looks or acts like their parents.]

(485)

ⲕⲓⳟ ⲅⲓⲧⲧⲓⲕⲕⲁ ⲉⲛⲛⲓ ⲟⲩⲡⲧⲁⲛⲛⲁ ⲟⲕⲕⲉ̄ⲛ.
Kid gittikka enni urtanna okkeen.
He who carries a heavy stone puts it on his head.

[Advice to think twice before doing something that may have heavy consequences.]

(486)

ⲕⲓⳟ ⲱⲉ̄ⲕⲕⲁ ⲥⲟⲕⲕⲁ ⲧⲓⲕⲕⲁⲛⲅⲟ̄ⲛ ⲥⲉⲅⲉⳟ ⲱⲉ̄ ⲫⲁⲗⲁⲕⲓ̄ⲛ.
Kid weekka sokka tikkangoon seged wee falakiin.
Whenever you lift a stone, a scorpion comes out.

[Advice to avoid dealing with certain people.]

(487)

ⲕⲟ̄ⲅⲁ ⲕⲟⲩⲛⲓ ⲅⲁⲣⲓ̄ⲃⲁⲅⲙⲟⲩⲛⲛⲁ.
Kooga kuni gariibangmunna.
He who has kin will not become a stranger.

[Advice not live or work too far away from your kin.]

(488)

ⲙⲁⲗⲗⲉⲗⲗⲁ ⲥⲟⲩⲕⲕⲁ ⳟⲁⲫⲓ̄ⲛ.
Mallella sukka dafiin.
He involves himself in everything.

[Says about someone who sticks his nose in everything.]

(489)

ⲱⲁⲗⲗⲟ ⲗⲉⲕⲓⲛ ⲉⲗⲧ̄ ⲙⲟ̄ⲗⲁ.
Wallo lekin elii moola.
Today is closer (better) than tomorrow.

[Advice not to postpone work.]

(490)

ⲟⲩⲧⲧⲟ̄ⲩ̄ⲛ ⲁⲥⲥⲁⲣⲣⲁ ⲕⲓⲯⲉ̄ⲗⲉⲕⲓⲛ ⲉⲅⲉⲇⲓⲛ ⲇⲟⲩⲱⲱⲓ ⲱⲉ̄ⲗⲗⲁ ⲕⲓⲯⲓⲕⲁⲛ ⲅⲉⲛⲁ.
Uttuun assarra kinynyeelekin egedin duwwi weella kinynyikan gena.
It is better to be tired of an old sheep than being tired of the children of others.

[Advice to take care of your own.]

(491)

ⲟⲩⲥⲟⲩⲣⲓⲛ ⲇⲉⲣⲁⳝⲅⲁ ⲛⲁⲓ̈ⲅⲁ ⲱⲉⲕⲕⲁⲧⲓⲱⲱⲁ?
Usurin jerahga nayga shekkatiwwa?
To whom we complain for the pain in our ass?

[Difficulty complaining of disobedience of sons.]

(492)

ⲇⲟ̄ⲅⲥⲁⲛ ⲙⲁⲗⲗⲉ̄ⲕⲁ ⳝⲁ ⲥⲓⲗⲗⲓⲛⲁ.
Joogsan malleeka fa sillina.
What they[47] grind, they[48] will scatter all.

[Advice to parents to act responsibly, lest the children carry the burden.]

---

47 I.e., the parents.
48 I.e., the children.

(493)

тōрēɴ ɴōρκōɴ ορгοɴ, ψιβιριɴ ɴōρκōɴ καβοɴ.
Tooreen noorkoon orgon, shibirin noorkoon kabon.
The owner of a spade was hungry, the owner of the basket ate.

> [Said when someone gets the profit of what others worked for.]

(494)

торβαρ гαρρι cīттιλα Διггιɴ.
Torbar garri siittila dingngin.
A bad farmer fights in the hay.

> [Said when someone destroys his own work because of their carelessness or stupidity.]

(495)

торδōροɴ Φαλτι гācιϳα.
Torjooron falti gaasiya.
He who interferes comes out with difficulty.

> [Advice that what you start you have to end.]

(496)

теме мαc темер ōусιɴαɴ κογμβακικαɴ ɴōг тαɴɴιɴ тōγλ αραгιɴ.
Teme mas temer uusinan kumbakikan noog tannin tuul aragin.
A good neighbor dances inside his house even when the bad neighbor beats his drums.

> [Advice to be kind and tolerant.]

(497)

ⲧⲟⲩⲥⲥⲓⲧⲁⲛ ⲙⲁⲣⲟⲓⲁ.
Tussitan maaroya.
His fart is a fertilizer.

[Said about someone who is very lucky.]

(498)

ⲟⲩⲃⲟⲩⲣⲧⲓ ⲧⲁⲕⲕⲁ ⲫⲓⲣⲙⲉⲛⲕⲁⲛ ⲕⲟⲗⲗⲟⲩⲙⲟⲩⲛⲛⲁ.
Uburti takka fiirmeenkan kollumunna.
Ash does not get stuck with whom does not transport it.

[Advice that evil only affects those who commit it.]

(499)

ⲟⲩⲅⲙⲉ ⲍⲁⲣⲁⲃⲁ ⲧⲁⲛⲅⲁ ⲟⲅⲟⲣⲙⲟⲩⲛⲛⲁ.
Ugmee haraaba tannga ogoormunna.
The owl does not forget his ruin.

[Saying that people with bad habits will fall back into them.]

(500)

ⲟⲩⲛⲛⲁⲣⲓⲛⲁⲛ ⲟⲩⲕⲕⲓ ⲛⲉⲇⲁ.
Unnariinan ukki neeja.
The ear who gives birth is deaf.

[Advice to choose the right moment to give advice, not when someone is preoccupied.]

References

ABDEL-HAFIZ, A.S. [Abdu al-Hafz]. *Nahw muhawala li kitabat alugha al-Nubiyya* [Towards an Attempt to Write the Nubian Language]. Cairo, 1998.
ABEL, H. *Eine Erzählung im Dialekt von Ermenne (Nubien)*. Leipzig, 1913.
AYOUB, Abd al-Rahman. *The Verbal System in a Dialect of Nubian*. Linguistic Monograph Series II. Khartoum: Sudan Research Unit, University of Khartoum, 1968.
BADR, Muhammad Mutwalli. *Al-lugha al-Nubiyya* [Study in Nubian Language]. Cairo: Dar misr lil-tiba, 1955.
———. *Hikam wa amthāl al-nuba* [Anecdotes and Proverbs of Nubia]. Khartoum: Institute of African & Asian Studies (IAAS), University of Khartoum, 1978.
———. *Igra bi al-nubiyya (Nubiin nog gery)* [Read in Nubian]. Khartoum: Institute of African & Asian Studies (IAAS), University of Khartoum, [1978].
BELL, H. *Place-names in the Belly of Stones*. Khartoum: Sudan Research Unit, University of Khartoum, 1970.
BROWNE, G.M. "Notes on Old Nubian." *Bulletin of American Society of Papyrologists* 16, no. 4 (1979): pp. 249–256.
BURCKHARDT, J.L. *Travels in Nubia*. London: John Murray, 1819.
CADALVENE, E. de, and J. de BREUVERY. *L' Egypte et la Turquie, de 1829 à 1836, vol. 2: Égypte et Nubie*. Paris, 1836.
GRIFFITH, F.Ll. "Some Old Nubian Christian Texts." *The Journal of Theological Studies* 10, no. 40 (1909): pp. 545–551.
———. *The Nubian Texts of the Christian Period*. Berlin: Verlag der Königlichen Akademie der Wissenschaften, 1913.
HĀSHIM, Al-Hādi H., and A.L. WHEELER [A. Cartwright]. *Nobinga Kull* [Learn Nubian]. Khartoum: Nobatia Society, 1997.
HASHIM, M.J. *Contribution of Nubian Language Speakers to the Development of Their Writing System: Insights Arising from Nubian Literacy Classrooms*. PhD Thesis, School of Language and Area Studies, University of Portsmouth, 2006.

———. *Nubian Orthography*. Cairo: Nubian Studies & Documentation Centre, 2008.

KABBARA, Mukhtar Khalil. *Nubiinga kull [Learning the Nubian Language]* Cairo: Nubian Studies and Documentation Center, 1999.

———. *Nubiinga sikkir faaywa? [How Do We Write the Nubian Language?]*. 1st edn. Cairo: Nubian Studies and Documentation Center, 1997.

KHALIL, M. [Kabbara]. *Wörterbuch der Nubischen Sprache.(Fadidja/Mahas-Dialekt)*. Warsaw, 1996.

LAUCHE, G. "A Contribution to the History of K.R. Lepsius, Translation of the Gospel of Mark into Mahas." *The International Conference of Meroitic & Nubian Studies*. Nice, 1996.

LEPSIUS, K.R. *Nubische Grammatik: Mit einer Einleitung über die Völker und Sprachen Afrikas*. Berlin: Wilhelm Hertz, 1880.

———. *[The Gospel According to St. Mark Translated into the Nubian language: An Edition of R. Lepsius' version, Transliterated into Arabic characters by Theodor Irrsich]*. Alexandria, 1899.

REINISCH, L. *Die Nuba-Sprache*. Vienna: Wilhelm Braumüller, 1879.

ROCHEMONTEIX, M. de. *Quelques contes nubiens*. Cairo, 1888.

SCHÄFER, H., and K. SCHMIDT. "Die ersten Bruchstücke christlicher Literatur in altnubischer Sprache." *Sitzungsberichte der Königlichen Preussischen Akademie der Wissenschaften* 43 (1906): pp. 774-785.

SHERIF, M. [Mohyi al-Din Sharif]. *Fadijja Nubian Language Lessons: For English Speakers*. Unpublished manuscript. Cairo, 1995.

SIMON, A., ed. *Nordsudan: Musik der Nubier*. Berlin: Musikethnologische Abteilung, Museum für Völkerkunde Berlin, 1980.

STRICKER, B.H. "A Study in Medieval Nubian." *Bulletin of the School of Oriental Studies, University of London* 10, no. 2 (1940): pp. 439-454.

SUNBAJ, Y. *Al-qamus al-nubi [The Nubian Dictionary: English/Arabic/Kenzi-Dongolese and Nobiin]*. Cairo, 1998.

Werner, R. *Grammatik des Nobiin (Nilnubisch)* (Hamburg: Helmut Buske, 1987).

ZYHLARZ, E. 1928. *Grundzüge der Nubischen Grammatik im Christlichen Frühmittelalter (Altnubisch)*. Leipzig: Deutsche Morgenländische Gesellschaft, 1928.

Printed in the USA
CPSIA information can be obtained
at www.ICGtesting.com
LVHW011930300624
784307LV00002B/87

9 781685 710187